BECOME
A
FIT*PRENEUR*

RACHEL WITHERS

To my parents, who taught me to believe in my dreams and myself. To my sister who is my best friend. And to my children Gregory and Clara who always inspire me to be the best I can be.

Love you all x

About The Author

Rachel Withers is the founder and manager of the wildly successful fitness concept, BalletBeFit. As a former dancer who trained with the Royal Ballet, she brings her ballet training and knowledge of health and posture into the gym, to help women of all ages, shapes and sizes get and stay in excellent shape.

As a FITpreneur she has built a profitable business based on her passion for ballet. Rachel and her team of instructors now offer a range of fun and challenging fitness courses combining the benefits of ballet training with the fun of dancing.

Foreword

In this well-written and entertaining book, Rachel Withers — founder of the successful fitness concept, BalletBeFit — takes us through what it takes to become a FITpreneur and demystifies the secrets to success in the fitness industry.

Through the 12 chapters Withers kills many common myths that hinder budding FITpreneurs, and challenges any prejudices about starting a fitness business. Her easy-to-follow and compelling writing style makes the information packed into every page effortlessly sink in with the reader. She makes even the most complex business concepts accessible and simple to understand for everyone. The result is a book that can be read from start to finish in a day as the perfect preparation to starting your own business plan. Or every chapter can be used as an encyclopedia and checklist for FITpreneurs at all levels.

Over the course of around 90 pages, Rachel Withers goes in great detail on how to set up your own successful fitness business; what to do and what NOT to do. She details what you need to start and how to take the first step. You'll learn how you should define your vision and develop your own unique business plan and action plan.

Chapter by chapter she takes you through everything you need to know before starting a successful fitness business. From all the practical aspects of physically setting up your gym, formulating and executing your business plan, to breaking down the mental barriers which hold you back.

When you have completed the book you will have a much clearer understanding of how you can live out your passion, and even turn it into a profitable business. Rachel is motivating you to follow your dream and showing you that you can do it throughout the book.

The continuous encouragement, abundance of practical advice and frequent debunking of misconceptions makes for a great companion for not just making it in the fitness industry, but for any entrepreneurial efforts.

This book is nothing less than a **MUST-READ** for any aspiring FITpreneur who wants to make it in the fitness industry!

Contents

Introduction

The Fitness Industry is one of the most lucrative and rewarding areas for any modern entrepreneur to consider.

You may have a great passion for fitness and perhaps you are wondering if it could be possible to turn this passion into your actual profession. The answer is a resounding "Yes!" But how exactly do you set up your own fitness empire, and become what we will refer to in this book as a 'FITpreneur'? The purpose of this book is to address that specific question.

Perhaps you're one of those people who look at other FITpreneurs and wonder what the great secret is behind their success. You may have seen people who operate their own gym and envied them for the incredible privilege of working in that environment every day. Perhaps you grew up in a family where your parents worked for the same company all of their lives, without ever amassing any significant amount of wealth. Before you read the contents of this book, you should be prepared to leave some of your prejudices behind, especially those which you may have inherited from your own family and friends. If that seems like a hard thing to do, simply ask yourself this question: How many of your family members and friends have their own successful businesses? The answer is probably that none of them do. This means that their ideas and advice about your decision to become a FITpreneur are probably not very reliable.

Once you are ready to let go of your previous notions of business and what it might take to become a FITpreneur, you are ready to read this book. Many people have tried to discover the secret of setting up their own successful fitness business and if you are one of them, I have good news for you. There is indeed a great secret which will enable you to become a successful FITpreneur, if only you can make it your own. But this secret is not floating somewhere out there and it is not to be found in a secret formula or a magic elixir.

The secret is inside you!

You see, the universe has conspired to place some incredible abilities and skills inside your spirit. When you were born, those skills, passions and abilities became a part of your physical body and you have always carried them with you ever since you were young. The secret is to find a way of making your inner passion for fitness your entire life purpose. If you follow the steps in this book, you will soon discover that your dreams and visions can actually materialise before your very eyes, and at a much quicker rate than you ever dreamed possible. All it requires is your time, faith and action.

You don't need any additional education or great wealth to start your own fitness business. All you need is a definite vision, backed up by a business plan and a plan of action. As you read through the chapters of this book, you will realise that you need to change your entire way of thinking before you will ever become the kind of individual who might ultimately have their own business. You will have to address some of the incorrect ways of thinking which you may have become accustomed to and you will need to reprogram your mind so that your thoughts become a conduit for the positive energies of the universe. You will also have to take some practical steps to set up your fitness business in such a way that you align yourself with the positive energies around you. Everything must work together, in harmony, towards the attainment of your ultimate vision.

I encourage you now to take a deep breath, sit back and start reading this book. Make sure to revisit any chapters when you feel the need to do so. You can even read through the entire book a number of times, if required. Now is the time to start renewing your mind and to prepare your spirit for the changes which need to be made before your dreams will become a reality. Do all of this correctly, and you will soon be on your way to becoming a FITpreneur!

CHAPTER ONE

What does it take to become a FITpreneur?

The image which comes to mind for most people, when they think about having their own fitness business, is that of a man with incredible muscles who trains all of his clients to become exactly like him.

Even if this is not the way you seriously think about the concept of becoming a FITpreneur, you might still feel intimidated by the idea of owning your own fitness business. It is time to learn an important lesson – anyone who really believes in their own vision of having a fitness business can become a FITpreneur!

One of the most important lessons which you need to learn very early on if you're hoping to become a financially independent FITpreneur is that simple, hard work will not necessarily get you there. Too often we fall into the trap of believing the classical mantra which has been forced down our throats from a young age, that the only way to make money is to work hard and consistently at your job. Just ask yourself the following question: How many of the people who kept forcing that mantra down your throat ever started their own fitness business? Their answer is probably not that many of them, if any at all.

The passion for fitness that you were born with, the dreams that you have always carried in your heart and the ideals you have espoused from a young age; those are often your best opportunities of making large sums of money. If you really want to become a FITpreneur you will have to tap into your true passion and understand that this is the gift which the universe has bestowed upon you.

{ **It's never too late to become a FITpreneur. All that is needed is some faith, hope and determination!** }

You might think that it is too late, or that you are too far gone to rekindle the passion you once had to own your own fitness business. But it's never too late to change your present course and ultimately become a FITpreneur!

Perhaps you once dreamed about opening an international chain of high-end, luxury gyms. But now you find yourself stuck in a 9-to-5 job where you don't even earn enough money to pay for the rent and monthly expenses. Don't despair! Many people in your position have pulled themselves up from the bootstraps, at a relatively advanced age, and managed to still make all of their original dreams come true by starting their own business. All that is needed is some faith, hope and determination.

Now that we have taken a brief look at the kind of belief that is required to become a FITpreneur, it would be good to more narrowly define what we mean by the very concept of *'being a FITpreneur'*. Obviously, if you live in a country where the local population generally believe in working out and going to the gym, the definition will be slightly different from a country where there are almost no gyms. You will need to create a level of fitness aspiration which is above the average level in your country, so that people will understand that they are getting something above average when they come to your gym. The reason why it is important to make this distinction, is to ensure you have a clearly defined aim and purpose when you set out on your journey of becoming a FITpreneur. When you know exactly what level you're aiming to achieve, it is easier to take concrete steps to achieve it. Once you have clearly defined your goals and plans, you are in a far better position to make them come true and the prospects of becoming a FITpreneur are exponentially increased.

All of the above considerations answer, to a certain degree, the question posed by the heading of this chapter, namely: *What does it take become a FITpreneur?* In the first instance, it requires accurate planning and a clearly defined strategy.

It should be clear to you by now that you are going to need a careful balance between your idealistic dreams and the very concrete strategies required to make them come true. Too often, people who want to have their own business are either extremely idealistic or only very practically inclined. Neither of these two approaches, practiced in isolation, will get you the desired result. You will need to be the kind of person who has their head in the clouds and his feet firmly planted on the ground, if you're going to ever become a FITpreneur.

Take a moment and try to imagine what it would be like to be a FITpreneur. Your mind immediately conjures up the kind of images popularly associated with people who are business owners. In your mind's eye, you see people having fun on deep-sea yachts, gambling in casinos across the world and driving around in Ferraris. Even though these images are not necessarily inaccurate or untrue, they do not necessarily give you a fair reflection of the average lifestyle and characteristics of a FITpreneur. Studies have shown that the number one characteristic shared by most successful business owners, is actually that of frugality. This means that, more than anything else, these people actually go out of their way to save money, rather than lavishly spending it. The person living right next door to you, despite the fact that he might appear to be an unassuming, average person, might actually be a business owner who simply saves his money and spends it wisely.

While we're discussing what it takes to become a FITpreneur, it is also important to stand still for a moment and consider what it takes to remain a FITpreneur. Too many people think that, once they have created a successful fitness empire, they can have an expensive lifestyle and buy all the lavish gifts and luxuries they want, without ever giving a second thought to the question of money or working ever again. They are wrong. Have you ever heard those stories of people who win the lottery? So many times you can pick up a newspaper and read how lottery winners spent their entire fortune in no more than a number of weeks or months! It is surprisingly easy to spend a million pounds; much easier than you may think. This is why it is very important to decide what you will do with your money once you have attained your goal of becoming a successful FITpreneur.

{ You need a role model, someone you can look up to and emulate! }

This is the point where it is helpful to start thinking about the kind of people you would like to emulate in your quest of becoming a FITpreneur.

Perhaps there is a health conscious man living in your area and you know that he's a FITpreneur. Look at the way he lives, what he does to stay healthy and the way that he spends his money. Does he go over the top and splash his cash without a second thought for the cost of such extravagance? Or is he more of a levelheaded person who spends his money wisely? Chances are, as soon as you start taking a closer look at this man who lives in your vicinity you will see that he actually gives a lot of careful thought to the way he expands his fitness business and spends his money. It might also be helpful to consider the way in which he presents himself. Is he arrogant, or is he more of a confident, straightforward person? You will probably find that, whilst most business owners have a lot of confidence in the way they present themselves and the decisions they make, they are seldom arrogant. Arrogant people tend to make unwise decisions and self-confidence should never be confused for arrogance.

Once you become a FITpreneur, you have to remember that it will be a brand-new experience for you. You'll have no previous track record or past history to refer to when you make your decisions as a FITpreneur. It would be very easy for you to make unwise decisions, even though they may appear to be wise ones. If you take all your money and buy new gym equipment, you may end up losing money when that equipment becomes outdated. You should not only look at examples of wise FITpreneurs around you, but also start thinking about employing a financial advisor to help you expand your fitness business wisely.

Another benefit of having a role model to look up to is that it will bring the entire concept of becoming a FITpreneur closer to home for you. Especially if your role model is someone whom you have seen, or met, in real life, you will no longer think of becoming a FITpreneur as some far-fetched, impossible goal to aspire to. It will seem more realistic to you, especially when you start finding out about the ways in which your role model actually started their fitness business. Once you understand the strategies and methods which your role model used, you will be able to start formulating your own strategies. It is important not to just copy what your role model did, but rather to try and discern some basic principles from their conduct. Make these principles your own and apply them to your own strengths and skills. In discerning the strategies of your role model, ask yourself the following questions. Did they start their fitness business immediately or did they first learn from someone else? Did your role model have a lot of luck, or just a lot of dedication? What kind of people did your role model employ to assist them in their quest of becoming a FITpreneur?

Through your study of someone whom you can look up to, you will start experiencing a vital change in the way you think. You will start aligning your own thoughts with the kind of thinking which your role model employed when they started their fitness business. Remember that a losing mindset will invariably produce losing results. In the same vein, a winning mindset will produce winning results and once you align your way of thinking with that of your role model, your prospects of creating your own fitness business will immediately increase exponentially.

{ ## The best time to become a FITpreneur is right now! }

At this point it is important to stress the fact that there has never been a better time for you to start your own fitness business as a FITpreneur. A hundred years ago or so, becoming a FITpreneur truly used to be a daunting aspiration, with very few ever being able to attain it. But today there is a lot of professional assistance and advice available. Opportunities for aspiring FITpreneurs to start their own fitness businesses in unsaturated areas of the market are everywhere and this is another great incentive for you to start out immediately on your quest of starting your own business.

Try to remove the restraints from the way you previously thought about becoming a fitness business owner. Perhaps you've only looked around your own city for opportunities of opening up your fitness business. Perhaps the only areas you ever considered were the ones close to you, while golden opportunities might exist in the next town. Now is the time for you to leave behind those mental constraints and to start looking out more widely for opportunities!

Let us stand still for a moment now at a concept which I have already touched on previously, namely *Investment*. I've already alluded to the fact that investment is one of the ways in which you may choose to dispose of your money once you have earned it. One common factor which almost all successful FITpreneurs have in common is that they invest wisely. Not only is investment a great way of holding onto your hard earned wealth, it is also way to keep regenerating new wealth. This is where the assistance of a legal advisor or an investment banker will be invaluable to you. They know exactly how to spread the risk across your entire investment portfolio, so that investment never becomes a way of losing money, but always remains a way of keeping it and making more.

Finally, you will notice that most of this chapter has been spent focusing on the very last stretch of your journey, namely what you will do once you have actually got your own successful fitness business. The reason for this is twofold. Firstly, it is important to start thinking about that future point in time before you ever get there. This way, you're not overwhelmed by sudden success and end up losing your money because you're so excited to have reached your goal that you don't have sufficient strategies to maintain your success. Secondly, you are also working on creating a positive mindset which will ultimately help you focus on the actual attainment of your goal. When you think about that point in the future when you have your fitness business, your mind starts focusing on success and the journey from here to there merely becomes the detail which needs to be filled in. You are programming your mind to accept the fact that your ultimate success is a foregone conclusion, and not a mere fantasy.

{ **Remember to stay patient.**
Don't start rushing towards the finish line }

The final thought which I want to leave with you under the heading of what it takes to become a FITpreneur, is the fact that you should remain patient. I'm not suggesting that you can only become a FITpreneur over a stretch of decades; merely that you should not ever get to the point where you start rushing towards your desired goal. One of the surest ways of making mistakes is when you lose your patience. Have you ever watched those programs on TV where poker players square off against each other in large poker tournaments? Often, when a certain player loses a couple of hands in quick succession, they will go on what is referred to in poker terms as *'full tilt'*. This means that, because they have lost a couple of poker hands in quick succession, the player becomes impatient and starts betting too much money, or playing too recklessly. Invariably, this results in that player wiping out the last of his winnings and being forced to leave the game. You don't want to be that player who goes in 'full tilt'. You don't want to get close to having your own fitness business and then, in an act of needless impatience, start rushing and making mistakes which ultimately prevent you from attaining your goal.

To summarise this chapter: Plan carefully, come up with strategies which employ the best of your skills and abilities and stay patient as you set out on your exciting journey of becoming a FITpreneur!

CHAPTER TWO

How to Design your Gym or Exercise Area

The principles we are going to discuss in this chapter apply to all kinds of businesses and areas of life, but even more so to the layout of exercise areas, where clients want to feel at ease during their workout.

You may already know something about the use of positive energy to help you achieve certain desired outcomes. To the uninitiated mind, the concepts of Feng Shui and Vastu energy may seem like magic, but I assure you that they are not.

Before we start exploring the precise ways in which positive energies may be utilised in order to help you become a FITpreneur, I want you to think back to some of the things you may have tried in your profession in the past. Perhaps you tried starting your own business and discovered that it simply never got off the ground because it lacked that magic ingredient. Maybe you had a business which started producing money, only to inexplicably fail after a couple of months. One of the possible explanations for such failure is not necessarily that you started the wrong business or lacked the skill to make a success of it, but rather that you never had the right energies working in your favour.

The entire universe is in a constant state of flux and so are the energies around you. Something which works for the first two months in a business can suddenly stop working and something which never produced results before can suddenly start producing results out of the blue. The secret behind this is the fact that there are energies at work and you will need to harness these energies and stabilise them if you ever hope to create the kind of forward momentum which will ultimately take you to the place where you have millions in the bank.

So what is Feng Shui and Vastu more precisely? Like I've already mentioned, these are not magic mantras or secret formulas for success. Rather, these principles are secret ways of influencing the forces around you and people in China and India have used them to their advantage for many centuries. Once you learn how to do the same, you will get that winning edge which has made so many people successful, even when their business and expertise were not necessarily better than that of their competitors. You are now about to learn about principles which, for centuries in ancient times, were jealously guarded as secrets to which only a very select few had access. Prepare your mind to be expanded and always remember that these principles are never to be abused for the wrong reasons. You should only use them to create a positive flow of energy in your business and to achieve the results which ultimately benefit not only yourself, but also your customers and others who come into daily contact with you.

Feng Shui, when translated, means '*Wind Water*'. Vastu, on the other hand, is the art of knowing the secrets of placement and design. Think of all those premises you have seen in movies where beautiful water fountains and windows have been placed carefully so that the entire room has a feeling of almost paradisiac wind and water balance. These premises have been designed according to the principles of Feng Shui and Vastu to achieve the maximum exploitation of energy. In other words, the premises with these kinds of designs were not accidents; they were specifically designed to achieve the maximum effect of positive energy for those who work in them. Basically, when you start learning about the optimum design and placement of wind and water elements on your premises, you are taking your first steps to bring the forces of the universe in alignment with your efforts and help you achieve your ultimate aim. This is not magic, but simply a skill which has been developed over centuries and is now available to you.

It would be impossible to explain, in just a couple of pages and paragraphs, all of the principles and secrets which comprise the entire field of knowledge which we refer to as Feng Shui and Vastu. Just like with financial investment, it would be best to consult a specialist in these fields so that you gain the expert help required when making these principles a part of your business design.

{ **The journey of a thousand miles begins with just one step** }

When you set out to create a business where you will ultimately have staff working in perfect harmony to achieve the desired end result, you need to be patient and understand that everything cannot be done in one day. Achieving perfect Feng Shui and Vastu balance, and effect the optimum placement of all the objects and energies in your business space will be a process. It can only be finalised and achieved through a long period of experimentation and constant improvement.

To better understand the principles of Feng Shui and Vastu, you should think of it as a skill which can slowly be learned and acquired in order to help you create a real relationship with your environment. Many people design their premises and business premises in such a way that it may appear to be very practical and efficient, yet they neglect to pay attention to the flow of energy through the place. This results in a premises where the staff never seem to settle down and really focus on their work. There is consistent distraction and the ultimate productivity level of such a premises never reaches its optimum peak. Yet, on the other hand, a premises may appear to be relatively humble insofar as high-tech equipment is concerned, yet it may be highly efficient insofar as the flow of energy is concerned. Such a premises, where Feng Shui and Vastu principles have been applied, will eventually be a place where the staff produce above average levels of productivity and ultimately contribute much more efficiently to the success of the business.

Ultimately, you want to use all of the energies around you in such a way that they become your partners and help you to attract wealth. Have you ever wondered why it is that some people just seem to get all the lucky breaks and all the most lucrative contracts in their business? I assure you that this is not by reason of luck, but rather by means of their alignment with the energies around them. They have learned how to create a harmony in their place of work which ultimately helps them attract those lucky breaks which no one else seems to get. The secret is to get yourself into a place where you have the same harmony with the energies around you. Some people may dismiss this part of the book which you're reading now as 'hocus-pocus' or daydreaming, but they do so at their own expense. These principles are nothing new and they have been tried and tested throughout many centuries with great success. The only question you need to ask yourself is whether you want to slug away and compete with your competitors without any real hope of gaining an edge over them, or whether you want to employ these secret principles and gain an edge which none of your competitors will ever have or understand.

Without going into too much detail here about the exact way in which you can align the objects and energies on your premises in accordance with Feng Shui and Vastu principles, I will outline just a couple of aspects to give you an idea of what the practical application of these principles encompass. You should understand that each direction on your premises has its own unique quality and energy characteristics. One might even refer to these directions or energies as *frequencies*. A compass may be used to ascertain each specific direction and the appropriate way of directing the energies that flow in those directions. Feng Shui is not a stagnant discipline, but rather something which has developed into many different styles, the same way that Kung Fu and martial arts have developed into different styles in ancient China. Each one of the different styles of Feng Shui has its own unique characteristics, but they all have the same ultimate aim, namely to direct the energies around you in such a way that you harmoniously work in alignment with the powers of the universe towards your ultimate purpose.

Once you get into the habit of looking at your gym or business environment according to the flow of energy through it, rather than simply considering the importance of getting the latest high-tech equipment and computers, you will start forming an understanding and spiritual sensitivity to the entire concept of Feng Shui. After a while, you will begin to see things in a spiritual and energy-focused way, rather than being blinded by the mere physical character of those things which make up your business environment. All of this is part of the essential learning process, which will ultimately help you gain that winning edge which we have alluded to earlier. The degree of dedication which you show in applying the principles discussed in this chapter will determine just how much of a winning edge you eventually acquire, so please do not skip over any of the important aspects which are discussed here.

Now that we have taken a look at the esoteric side of Feng Shui and Vastu energy, it is necessary to start bringing these principles closer to home and to illustrate, by means of practical examples, exactly what these principles entail with regards to your everyday working and home environment. Have you ever entered a kitchen where lots of dirty dishes have been left in the sink and the entire place reeks of old food and rotten eggs? Can you imagine what kind of negative energies any person will encounter when they enter such an untidy and unhygienic kitchen? You don't have to know anything about the ancient arts of Feng Shui and Vastu to understand that any person who enters such a dirty place will immediately pick up 'bad vibes'. The same goes for your gym or business premises. Even if you have all of the latest gym equipment and the whole place appears to be reasonably tidy, your customers may still be put off if they find it difficult, for example, to move in between the exercise apparatus. They may not even know why, but they may feel as if they are picking up negative vibes and not enjoying the experience of working out. This is not a reflection, necessarily, of the technical or hygienic qualities of your business space, but rather a reflection on the failure to achieve a positive flow of energy through the place. On the other hand, if a customer should enter a gym and the first thing they see is a beautiful, peaceful waterfall with a pleasant breeze circulating through the place, they will immediately feel welcome and are more likely to be willing to sign up permanently. This, in its simplest form, is an explanation of the difference between a place where negative energies prevent you from achieving success and a place where Feng Shui and Vastu principles give you the winning edge and attract your clients to sign up with your fitness business.

There is more at work in these principles than merely the energies out there in your workout space. Feng Shui and Vastu also provides a reflection of your inner energies and the inner balance which you have achieved. For example, a person who has an untidy house is normally the kind of person whose general outlook on life is also untidy. Such a person is more likely to be careless in their everyday decisions. In the same vein, a person with a tidy house and a balanced flow of energy through their business space, is a person who has the same kind of balance inside. In other words, in achieving a natural flow of Feng Shui and Vastu energies through your business environment you are also achieving and reflecting the inner peace and balance which you've achieved inside your spirit. People will be attracted to this inner and outer balance they see in you and, before you know it, you will start noticing a definite upswing in the general trend of your business volume.

It is important to understand that there are both positive and negative energies to be found in the study of Feng Shui. As we have discussed before, a person who fails to fully utilise and direct the flow of positive energy through their business environment will often allow the presence of negative energies in its place which, in turn, will deflect customers rather than attract them.

In practice, Feng Shui practitioners will use art, astrology, interior design, tasteful décor and various other means to achieve their ultimate aim, namely to ensure the sensible and positive flow of energy through the workplace. Water features and air ventilation will also play a very important part in the greater design of your workplace.

Feng Shui and Vastu principles extend towards other areas of your life as well, namely your marriage, relationships, sexual happiness and general well-being. It is not too surprising to consider Feng Shui has now become an almost household word in most modern businesses. CEO's and managers have all experienced, firsthand, how successful the application of these ancient principles can be in modern times. One of the most striking examples where we find an application of Feng Shui and Vastu principles is the modern boardroom, where square tables of old have now been replaced, in almost all instances, by round and oval tables in order to avoid the onset of conflict. When one is seated at a table without any edges there is less chance of considering the person on the opposite end as your opponent. A round table creates the impression of everyone being seated next to each other and makes everyone present feel as if they are working together in harmony.

{ ## Make sure you apply these Principles in all areas of your Life }

Remember that the discipline of Feng Shui is not to be confined exclusively to the workplace. It would make no sense, for example, to start practicing yoga and then to neglect other areas of your life, such as a healthy diet. You may spend three hours a day doing yoga and destroy all of it by walking to the burger hut and buying yourself three hamburgers every day, right after yoga practice. In the same way, you should not attain a beautiful, balanced flow of energy in the workplace and then return home, only to let go of all those principles. Make Feng Shui a discipline which you apply in both your workplace and in your home environment. You will find that it will not only improve your business relations and general professional success, but also improve the general harmony in your home.

It will be helpful, at this point, to take a look at some of the principles of yoga, as it will shed more light on the practical mechanics of Feng Shui and Vastu. In yoga, practitioners are taught that there are certain energy centres located all over the human body and they may be accessed and maximised in order to make the body a more harmonious instrument. These energy centres are called chakras. In Feng Shui and Vastu, the same principles apply. There are certain energy points in your business environment. Once you understand that energy flows between these points, you will see that it operates much the same way as the chakra energy points in a person's body. For example, one of the energy points on your premises will be the chair that you sit in. Another energy point will be the chair opposite your desk, the place where important people might sit when you are discussing business deals with them. Between these two chairs there will be a natural flow of energy which can either be positive or negative, depending on whether you have successfully applied the principles of Feng Shui and Vastu to maximize the energy flow between these points. If your desk is cluttered and full of unnecessary papers and other distracting items, you will most probably find yourself with a negative flow of energy between these two important points on your premises. On the other hand, if you have a small water fountain on your table and a bonsai tree opposite it, this will create a beautiful flow of positive energy and an inviting environment within which to conduct your business dealings.

Many businessmen also use gemstones and other powerful spiritual objects to enhance the positive flow of energy in their workplace. Even the disciplines of astrology and spiritual enlightenment may be used to further enhance the positive energy in your working environment. Powerful talismans may also be used, in the same way that you might use gemstones to create a natural harmony and balance around you. When it comes to astrology, you might want to start studying the different phases of the moon. For example, when the moon is waxing it is generally not a good time to start the planning and implementation of new business proposals and projects.

As we continue to discuss the ways in which the energy flow around you can be directed and balanced, you will start to form an understanding of the basic principle which underlies all of these disciplines, namely that the entire universe consists of energy. The gemstones, talismans, water features, air ventilation, art, decor and other practical ways in which Feng Shui practitioners practice their art all have one thing in common: All of it enhances the natural and harmonious flow of energy in the Universe in such a manner that it ultimately benefits your business in a practical way.

Even if you're in the fitness business, you will still need a premises where you can meet with prospective investors and business partners. When people come to see you concerning business related issues, they might initially be nervous about the prospects of the encounter. After all, once you start doing the kind of business where millions of dollars or pounds are involved, it is only natural that there will be a slight trepidation on behalf of those people who come to discuss such large business ideas with you. Now, if you do absolutely nothing to make these people feel comfortable, once they are seated across from you at the premises, you're probably going to make them feel even more nervous. If, on the other hand, you have an premises which has been optimally arranged according to the principles of Feng Shui and Vastu energy application, you're going to put your prospective business partners at ease and this will be conducive to much more successful business dealings. Dealing with a relaxed person is much easier than trying to deal with a nervous business partner.

You ultimately want to create a friendly and harmonious atmosphere where all people involved with your business can relax and produce their best. Not only will this approach enhance your dealings with prospective business partners, but it will also help your staff and workforce to perform better. People tend to deliver their best when they are relaxed and positive. No one likes to work in an environment where they feel nervous about their performance, and this is why the positive flow of energy through your workplace is so important if you want to get the best possible assistance from your staff.

It is important not to think of any of the disciplines which we have discussed here in isolation. It would do you little good if you spend a lot of time getting peaceful art and beautiful paintings for your premises, whilst neglecting the installation of suitable water and wind features in terms of Feng Shui practice. In the same vein, it would do you no good to get beautiful gemstones and powerful talismans to enhance the positive flow of energy in your workplace, if you do not also make sure that you have applied all of the comprehensive principles of Vastu placement and coordination with regards to these items.

Another important consideration is the fact that it might cost you considerable amounts of money to eventually create a Feng Shui and Vastu friendly environment, within which to perform your daily work duties. Bear in mind that Rome was not built in one day and that it is always possible to start small and later enhance the application of these principles, as more funds become available to improve your premises.

Let us spend a few moments now to discuss some more practical examples of things which can be attended to on your premises, in order to take the first steps of making your workplace more Feng Shui and Vastu friendly. None of the following steps will necessarily cost you a lot of money. You can attend to them without spending too much cash as you start out. When you start looking at these aspects, you might quickly realise that you have actually made a lot of mistakes in some of the following areas. Do not be too hard on yourself when you see these mistakes; rather be grateful for the fact that you are now taking the very important steps of eliminating these negative, energy draining problems from your life and workspace. Also bear in mind that none of the following pointers are to be taken in isolation. You will need to address all of these areas as a whole, to ensure that a comprehensive and balanced flow of positive energy is created and maintained throughout your business environment.

Electrical equipment

Few things will clutter up your workplace and create more negative energy than open electrical wires and electrical equipment lying around. Not only does this look untidy, it is also a very powerful way for negative energies to be conducted and directed through your workplace. It will catch the eye and immediately distract people from the places where you want them to focus, so make sure that you don't have any untidy electrical cables and other equipment lying around on your premises.

Remove dangerous objects

This includes all sharp objects and pointed ornaments. Not only are these things physically dangerous to clients who are trying to do a workout, they are also conductors of negative Feng Shui energy and any experienced Feng Shui practitioner will tell you that such objects need to be avoided at all costs. Think back to the principles we have discussed earlier, concerning the replacement of square conference tables with more rounded ones. You will quickly see that the basic principles are the same when it comes to the removal of objects with sharp and pointed shapes, as such objects are conductors of negative energy.

Plants

Be sure to make a point of only keeping plants in your gymnasium that are green and luscious in appearance. Very few things will create more negative energy than a weathered plant. When you have dead plants in your exercise area it creates the impression that things are dying around you and that it is not a healthy space. Make sure that every plant you have is luscious, beautiful and green.

Basic cleanliness

Make sure that your premises are spotless and dust free. This principle does not require too much explanation, as you will probably be aware of the fact that most people will consider a dirty exercise area to be a negative influence on their ability to pursue greater health and fitness. Apart from this obvious fact, a dirty business environment will also conduct negative Feng Shui energy.

Round, smooth objects

As we have seen before, objects with rounded edges and rounded shapes are far more conducive to friendly, non-combative energy than square objects. The first place where you will find the opportunity of applying this principle is the shape of your reception desk and entrance area. You can also design the basic layout of your gym and exercise area in circular shapes. Not only will this look more pleasing to the eye, it will also facilitate the smooth flow of positive energy throughout the entire space.

Cover pointed objects

Sometimes it won't be possible to permanently remove all of the square objects from your premises. However, if you were to ultimately leave these square objects out in the open, they will gather what is known as 'poison arrows' of negative energy and also reflect that same negative energy towards anyone who happens to be in the room. Objects which fall into this category are bookshelves, books, and other square objects. These objects should, as far as possible, be covered by cloth or other means.

Mirrors

We already have discussed the importance of beautiful, peaceful paintings for your premises. Not only will beautiful pieces of art enhance the general appearance of your premises, they will also become conduits for the flow of positive energy. But don't forget to also remove unnecessary mirrors on your premises and home. A mirror against the wall will make the room appear to be larger and it will add a certain surprise quality to the general feel of the space you find yourself in. These can be very powerful conduits of negative energy, as they create hollow spaces and a general feeling of being lost. It is far better to stick with a few pieces of selected art, which will give you a far greater sense of calmness than the surprising effect of a large mirror against the wall.

The placement of exercise equipment

It is important to place your equipment in such a way that it creates an impression of harmony whenever someone enters your premises. Make sure that every object is arranged in a way that pleases the eye and allows for the effective flow of positive energy.

Remove straight lines

By now you will have a good understanding of one of the very basic principles of Feng Shui, namely the idea that rounded shapes and objects are desirable above square, pointy objects. Apart from furniture and other items on your premises, there will be other lines and designs which may still retain the impression of straight lines and sharp edges. Examples of these are the shutters on your window, the shape of the room and the shape of the windows. Obviously, you cannot change the shape of the room or the shape of the windows, so other techniques should be employed to soften their straight lines and sharp edges. Some of the ways in which this can be achieved is by hanging gemstones, crystals and other Feng Shui items on your premises, as well as the introduction of beautiful shapes, such as elegant lamps and soft curtains, to break up the remaining straight lines on your premises.

Your bed at home

It is important not to place your bed at home right opposite the door in your bedroom, as this will obstruct the natural flow of positive energy into one of the most important rooms in your environment. After all, the bedroom is the place where you will be spending more than a third of your time sleeping, and if you attract a negative flow of energy in this environment it will not be conducive to your general sense of well-being and success.

Lighting

Once you have taken care of the basic ideas of placement, balance, Feng Shui energies and correct Vastu placement, you should also spend some time thinking about proper lighting for all of your rooms. Centuries of Feng Shui practice teach us that a low quality of lighting, or the absence of adequate lighting, always brings about the flow of negative energy, as dark shadows and inadequate lighting will inevitably bring about dark moods in yourself and everyone around you. A brightly lit room reflects positive energy and will also illuminate your entire being as long as you find yourself in it.

Composition

Another finishing touch which should be applied, once you have taken care of your Feng Shui and Vastu principles, is variation and proper composition of all the elements on your premises. Here you can use a little bit of originality and flair, for example by placing silver balancing scales on your wooden desk, or breaking up the monotony of the bookshelf by placing a luscious, green plant right on top of it.

Get proper rest

Returning for the moment to your home environment, it is important to drape your bedroom in natural canvas and to stick to white and cream colours for your bed. Not only does this look beautiful, it also brings about the flow of positive energy by virtue of the fact that lighter colours reflect more light and illuminate the entire room. In addition to white bedding, red and pink colours can also be used in the bedroom to add an element of passion.

The proper use of mirrors

We have already alluded to the fact that unnecessary mirrors against your walls should be removed, as they are conduits of negative energy. The proper use of mirrors are in cupboards, where they will enhance your dressing experience and preparation for the day. But do take care not to hang a mirror on the bedroom wall or to sleep in front of one, as this will bring about the flow of negative energy and, in some cases, even contribute to bad luck.

Stick with wood

Whenever possible, you should use wood instead of metal objects, as this is more natural and in keeping with general Feng Shui principles. For example, if you can hang wooden blinds in front of the window then do so and remove all metal blinds, to create a more natural atmosphere at your business premises.

The proper use of plants

As mentioned before, bonsai trees are an excellent choice for your premises. They create the impression of ancient wisdom and are wonderful conduits for the flow of positive energy throughout your business space. Use these, and other green plants, as often as possible and always make sure that all the plants in your working environment are property watered, as dried up and dying plants create a feeling of death and failure.

Make use of candles

A distinction should be drawn between the kind of candles which you burn at home and those which you use at the business premises. No candles should be used in the reception area of your business premises, unless your business is a spa or massage parlour. However, one or two white candles against the wall may enhance the flow of positive energy in your business environment. At home, especially in the bedroom, colours of red and pink are preferable for candles, as they signify romance and love.

Ornaments

When you decide to place ornaments around the premises and your home, follow the ancient wisdom of the Chinese and make use of turtles, dragons and the Phoenix. You may also use lions and doves, as all of these animals are associated with good luck and the positive flow of energy.

The proper use of gems

We have already discussed the proper use of gems at the premises, insofar as it promotes the positive flow of energy throughout your business environment. More specifically, you should try to use Jade stones, as these are highly favoured ornaments insofar as the practice of Feng Shui is concerned. You may also use rubies, emeralds and some selected varieties of crystal. None of these items are extremely expensive and they will definitely enhance your premises.

Air flow through the exercise area

As we have seen earlier, one of the elements of Feng Shui is actually wind and therefore it is important that you employ certain techniques to facilitate the smooth flow of air through your premises. However, air itself is not a visible element and therefore the proper airflow through your premises should be made more visible by the use of wind chimes. Not only does this create a pleasing and peaceful sound when the wind blows through the chime, it also makes people aware of the fact that there is a natural airflow and positive alignment of wind energy throughout your exercise area.

Water

The other element of Feng Shui which is of utmost importance, as mentioned earlier, is water. Small water features, such as miniature waterfalls, can be utilised with great effect on your premises and you should also consider the possibility of placing some of these in your reception area, as water provides a feeling of vitality and energy to your premises.

Computers screens

UV filters should be applied across all computer screens, not only to protect your eyes from the effects of continuous lighting, but also to avoid the flow of negative energy from the computer to yourself.

Flowers

Flowers, just like other plants, should always be fresh. Flowers can be used very effectively in the premises environment, as well as at home. There are no hard and fast rules as to which flowers you should use, but Lotus flowers are a highly favoured variation as they signify peace, spirituality and the principles of great passion. Make sure that you choose a variety of flower for your premises which is suitable to the rather harsh conditions of a business environment. The last thing you want is flowers that are wilted every morning when you arrive for work.

Crystal vases

Crystal is a very powerful item and throughout many centuries people have confirmed its intrinsic healing value. When you place crystal vases and bowls around your premises, you facilitate the flow of positive energy, by both the reflection of light on the crystal and through the general sense of well-being generated by the crystal's healing qualities. Crystal can be used in many variations, including the kind of crystals which may be hung in front of a window. There are many types of crystal and you should choose those which make the most sense for your premises, in combination with the other Feng Shui items which you have chosen.

Goldfish

Throughout the centuries, a small bowl with a goldfish or two inside has become a symbol of wealth and positive energy. Use some of these at your reception area and also inside your premises to create a sense of ancient wisdom, positive energy and general well-being.

Bowl with coins

Something else which you may place on your premises to attract wealth is a bowl with coins. This signifies the fact that you are making money and preparing yourself to become a FITpreneur.

{ **Make use of the powerful effects of Colour Therapy** }

Throughout the act of carefully placing various items and crystals around your premises, you should always bear in mind that colour is of utmost importance. Through the centuries wise people have studied the effects of certain colours on human mood swings and general well-being. The use of colour has always been a significant part of the traditions of yoga, especially as it improves the harmonious powers of the body and mind. The Chinese have a long line of tradition concerning the use of colour, as do the Egyptian and Greek societies.

One of the most important areas where colour therapy may be applied, is in the location and enhancement of energy centres or chakras. Once this has been done, colour therapy becomes more than a tool for emotional well-being, it also becomes a conduit for the attraction of wealth and positive energy at your premises.

The proper application and use of effective colour is a very important part of Feng Shui. As already discussed before, your bedroom at home should focus on the colours of passion, namely red and pink. At the premises, you should choose lighter colours to facilitate a feeling of positive energy and excitement. Also make sure that you have proper sources of light at the premises to further enhance the use of bright colours. At home, use green and blue colours in those rooms where you need a feeling of healing, calmness and peace.

Important colours for the attraction of clients

The most important colours for the attraction of new clients are gold and green. It goes without saying that gold is a good colour to use around the premises if you want to attract new business, as it signifies the possession and ultimate attainment of financial wealth in the form of gold itself. In conjunction with the use of golden colours, you should also employ the proper use of green colours.

This may be achieved by way of green flower leaves, as well as the use of green plants on your desk.

Spiritual colours

In many cultures of the world certain colours have long been associated with spirituality. Certain religions will make use of scarlet robes, whilst others prefer the use of white robes to signify spiritual purity and strength. It is recommended that you stick with white when it comes to your premises, to enhance a feeling of spirituality and spiritual strength. Not only should white be an important part of the colouring of your premises itself, you should also remember to wear white shirts and white handkerchiefs wherever possible. This will create a sense of spiritual purity and spiritual strength whenever people come to meet you at the premises.

Colour can be an important indication of spiritual prowess and it also has intrinsic spiritual qualities, especially insofar as aspects of healing are concerned. Throughout the centuries many studies have been conducted to illustrate how the correct use of colour may enhance healing and emotional well-being. The use of colour in the area of healing is so important that it takes its rightful place alongside traditional medicine, for example when it comes to the treatment of conditions such as depression and anxiety.

Remember that, in conjunction with the correct use of colour, bright lighting is a fundamental cornerstone of Feng Shui. White light consists of all the colours of the rainbow, condensed into one. When white light is broken up into its full spectrum, it contains every single colour imaginable. Therein lies a powerful truth, namely that a brightly lit premises ultimately reflects the idea that all of the colours in the universe have been properly channelled throughout your premises.

CHAPTER THREE

Use Your Mind
as a Fitness Power Tool

One of the most revolutionary concepts you will need to grasp if you are ever going to realise your dreams of setting up your own fitness empire, is to use your mind as a fitness power tool. This will allow you to impose your vision on the exercise area of your fitness business, as well as your trainers and other staff.

You have probably already heard of the concept of synergy. Synergy is a combination of the words *synchronise* and *energy*, thereby signifying exactly what it means, namely the proper application of energy in a synchronised fashion. When proper synergy has been achieved, there is a balance of Feng Shui energies. A person who has achieved synergy will find himself in a place where all of his skills and efforts are channelled successfully, in alignment with the positive powers of the universe.

One of the most important skills to master on your journey to becoming a FITpreneur, is to learn how to employ the creative power of your mind. You need to find a way of creating a synergy in your subconscious mind which will ultimately produce the results that you are seeking, namely the growth of your fitness business. This means that you will have to start programming and reprogramming your subconscious mind. Not all of the things you were taught as a child were correct or even positive. Think, once again, of all the incorrect teachings you may have received concerning the attainment of true wealth. So many people may have drilled it into you that only hard, repetitive work can ever produce success, that your subconscious mind may have started believing it. Yet, the truth is that a person who hates what he or she does for a living will never become successful doing it.

You need to train your mind to start thinking differently about work. Think back to the early cartoons that were drawn and how the creators of those first cartoons must have had incredible fun while they were creating their animations. I'm quite certain that they never went to work with a sense of hating what they did for a living. Yet, contrary to all of those incorrect teachings you may have received, these cartoonists ended up making millions, and even billions, whilst having fun at work!

It is absolutely essential that you get yourself into a mental space where you are the only one who controls the programming of your mind and subconscious thoughts. If you keep thinking the way everyone else does, you cannot expect to have better results than the average person around you. However, if you can train your mind to expect success and move towards it naturally, you will exponentially increase the prospects of attaining success and becoming a FITpreneur.

{ **The Mind is a mighty, Powerful Tool!** }

Make no mistake, your mind is the most important factor in the equation which will ultimately determine whether you ever attain the kind of success you have always dreamed of. If your mind remains stuck in traditional fables concerning the attainment of wealth, you will never create the kind of thinking patterns which will ultimately facilitate your successful journey towards the top. If, on the other hand, you can train your mind to become a powerful weapon of positive thought and energy, it will propel you towards the attainment of wealth and become your strongest weapon in the ultimate competition with your competitors in the marketplace.

How exactly can you start programming your mind in a positive way? The key is to keep speaking positive thoughts into your subconscious mind. You might do this by way of whispering positive things to yourself, such as *"I know I'm going to make it"*, or *"I'm the kind of person who always succeeds"*. This may sound and feel silly at first, but your mind is an incredible machine which is designed to ultimately accept those thoughts which are repeatedly entered into it. Keep saying these things to yourself until you start believing them. Once you believe these positive messages, your mind will start looking for ways of making them a reality and your subconscious mind will become like a secret computer inside your head, formulating brilliant plans to facilitate your journey towards wealth. You might go to sleep at night, perplexed by a certain problem you're experiencing at work, and wake up the next morning with the realisation that your subconscious mind has come up with an answer to that problem! But this will happen only if you train your mind to become your most valuable asset, rather than a conduit for negative energy.

Keep thinking and whispering those positive thoughts to yourself whenever you have the opportunity. You'll be astounded at how quickly your mind will eventually start accepting these positive reinforcements and uplifting messages.

One very important fact to keep in mind when you start programming your subconscious mind for success, is that you shouldn't just believe the positive messages to a certain degree. Unless you believe it one hundred percent, you're wasting your time. You have to get to a point where your mind acts like a computer which simply accepts the positive data which you are feeding into it, so that it can start programming your way to success on a subconscious level. Those subconscious plans will eventually find a way into your daily existence, but only if you have truly believed the positive messages in the first place.

Another thing to remember is that you cannot embark on this process of positive programming in a haphazard way. It would do you no good to start thinking a positive thought every now and then, whenever you feel bored or have nothing else to do. Approach it the same way you would approach the learning of a new skill, such as chess. If you really want to become a great chess player, you have to start from scratch and learn all of the great opening moves. You have to go through a period of repetition and daily study in order to become familiar with all of the various opening patterns on the chessboard, and only when you have really mastered the basics will you be able to move on to the next level. It works the same way with the positive programming of your mind.

First of all, you have to become familiar with your own thought processes. Ask yourself a number of questions to discover the patterns of your own thinking. When is your mind most likely to wander off into patterns of negative thinking? At what time of the day do you normally feel the most energetic? When are you most likely to feel positive about the prospects of making a success of your life? All of these questions, and the answers to them, will reveal to you a lot about your mental capacity and the way your mind works. For example, you may discover that you tend to be negative in the early hours of the day, as you might be a slow starter. Perhaps to become more positive towards the end of the day and even more energetic as the day progresses. Use this information to decide when it would be best for you to start programming your mind with positive thoughts. If you're one of those people who struggle to get started in the mornings and even experience patterns of negative thought early in the day, then those early hours are the most important time for you to reinforce your mind with positive messages. If, on the other hand, you tend to get negative towards the end of the day and lose your faith and hope as the day progresses, then you will obviously have to spend some time reinforcing your mind with positive thinking towards the end of your day.

It is important for you to realise that a lot of personal thoughts, which may have become cornerstones of your way of thinking, could be the result of careless words and things spoken to you when you were just a young child. Perhaps your parents told you that poverty runs in the family, or that you will have to earn your bread one day by doing hard, manual labour. Even though they may have meant well when they spoke this way, they might have ended up programming your mind to accept poverty as the norm. Studies have shown that almost all FITpreneurs who grew up in poverty have one specific thing in common, namely the fact that they never accepted that poverty as their ultimate destiny. All of them decided, from an early age, that they were going to do whatever was necessary to uplift themselves from those poor surroundings in which they grew up. Perhaps you are not living in poverty right now, but you may still have a poverty-stricken mindset and it is time for you to identify those negative thoughts which may have been injected into your mind as a young child, and then remove them.

Form a Mental Picture of Your Ultimate Fitness Empire

One of the most powerful ways of programming your mind for success, is to create a mental picture of the way you would like your financial empire to look one day. This includes the kind of car you want to drive, the house you want to live in and the kind of job you want to do. Don't worry if the mental picture your mind conjures up scares you somewhat by its sheer expansiveness. It might come as a surprise to you, but the picture which your mind comes up with when you think about success is actually something which the universe has placed there for you, as a roadmap towards your ultimate destiny. If you see something which you have never previously thought might be within your reach, don't let this become a stumbling block to you. Rather see it as a source of inspiration and start thinking what it would take for you to achieve the kind of success which goes with this mental picture of your ultimate financial empire.

Remember that the most important person who needs to believe in your vision is yourself. You cannot expect someone else to stand by your side and constantly reinforce your faith in yourself. Very often, the first people who hear about your vision for a fitness business will reject it and perhaps even scoff at your plans. This includes the bank manager, who might smile smugly when you explain to him why you need a loan from the bank. He might even tell you that your ideas are irrational and bound for failure.

You should know that these words and rejections can make or break you. If you accept the quick judgments which people, such as that bank manager, may make when you tell them about your plans, then you might as well let go of all your dreams. You will have to decide that you truly believe in your ideals and that you are going to achieve them, no matter what other people say about your intentions. This is why it is so important to absolutely believe those positive messages with which you reinforce your subconscious mind. Only if you believe those positive thoughts to the maximum, will you be able to withstand the kind of mental pressure which comes with the rejection of your ideas by others. Whilst we are using the example of the bank manager as a person you might approach for financing, it is important to start freeing your mind from the idea that banks are the only way to finance your financial future. What about putting together a careful brochure which outlines your plans and presenting it to prospective investors? You may find that investors could be the answer to the financing of your business, as they are often more adventurous in their outlook on financial endeavours than bank managers might be.

Self-Hypnosis

When most people hear the word hypnosis, they immediately think of those crazy TV shows where the hypnotist will call someone from the audience, placing them under hypnosis and then make them do funny things, such as taking off their shirt and acting like a monkey. But hypnosis isn't just for comedy. You might be surprised to hear that many self-made FITpreneurs have made extensive use of self-hypnosis in order to achieve the kind of positive programming of the subconscious mind which we have spoken about previously. You can also use the process of self-hypnosis the same way by employing the following two techniques, namely *Visualisation* and *Trataka.*

Visualisation of your Fitness Empire

The first way in which you may use hypnosis is by way of a process called visualisation. This means that you're going to take that mental picture which you have created of your fitness empire, truly focus on it and reinforce it with consciously repeated positive messages. The ideal time for you to do this is just before you go to bed.

When you are ready, make sure that you are not going to be distracted or disturbed by anyone else and make yourself comfortable on your bed. Once you are comfortable, start clearing your mind from all thoughts, especially any thoughts connected to negative experiences you may have had during the day. Start inhaling and exhaling very deliberately and very rhythmically. Try to slow down your breathing and to allow your body to relax as you do so. When you feel yourself relaxing, your body will start getting rid of all negative energies and this is when you will truly feel your mind clearing and becoming receptive to the ultimate visualisation which you're going to do.

Now you are ready for the next step. Keep breathing in and out rhythmically and start repeating a very specific, positive sentence to yourself, audibly. You should speak out as you exhale and you might say something like the following, *"I am successful and I possess a magnificent fitness empire."* Remember to take the whole process very seriously and to keep repeating that specific sentence for at least ten minutes or more while you inhale and exhale smoothly. If you do this correctly, the entire process will induce a state of semi-hypnosis and you will ultimately force your subconscious mind to accept the fact that you are a highly successful person who has been destined for great financial success.

Remember that this cannot be a once-off procedure. Just like we have discussed before, you need to repeat this process and make it part of your daily routine. Choose a time of the evening when you know you will not be disturbed and do the same thing every evening, without fail. After about thirty days, you will start noticing an incredible change in the way you think and, all throughout the day, you will reap the benefits of the visualisation which you have achieved through self-hypnosis.

Trataka

This is an ancient process, during which you bend down on your knees, or sit down cross-legged if there is some physical reason why you cannot bend down on your knees. Before you sit down, you should place a bright candle some distance away from you, approximately two feet. You may place the candle on a small table or something else, so that it is approximately at the same level as your eyes. Now, start breathing rhythmically, the same way you did with your visualisation exercises, and focus intently on the light of the candle. If you need to do so, close your eyes every now and then for a couple of seconds and then open them again. Visualise the energy of the candle light streaming into your body and keep breathing rhythmically and smoothly as you do so.

Now it is time to start repeating some positive thoughts to yourself, while you carry on looking at the candle and breathing smoothly. Choose a positive thought, such as, "*I am successful and successful in everything I do*," and speak it out softly while you continue with the entire procedure. Just like with the visualisation exercise, you should sit down at specific times during each day and repeat this process of *Trataka*. It will do you no good to do it once or twice and then expect incredible results. You will need to be faithful and committed to making this second step of self-hypnosis a part of your daily routine, if you really want to reap all the benefits which may be gained from it.

CHAPTER FOUR

Free Yourself by becoming a successful FITpreneur!

When you reach this part of the book you will already have a better idea of the concrete steps required to ultimately create your own fitness empire.

By now you have laid a firm foundation upon which you may start building your future success, provided you have studied and followed all of the initial steps in this book. You now understand the importance of visualising your success and programming your subconscious mind to accept that you will eventually achieve it. You have also used some of the practical advice to create a home and business environment where your positive energies can blend in with those of the universe to propel you to your ultimate success. Despite the fact that your focus will ultimately be on physical exercise and well-being, you will also have to pay attention to some established financial principles along the way.

The time has come for you to start taking practical steps towards achieving your ultimate goal of becoming a FITpreneur. It is good to take the preliminary steps and to spend the time reinforcing a pattern of positive thinking, but these are only the beginnings of your dream. Nothing will happen unless you also take concrete steps to make it a reality.

One of the first things you should understand is that you are responsible for your success. You can never get into a pattern of believing that there will be someone else to save you if things go wrong. Don't trust the bank manager, or family members, to come to your aid when you fall on hard times. You will have to learn to be frugal in your ways and to save as much money as you can along the way. Obviously, you're going to have certain expenses in setting up your fitness business, but hopefully you have some investors to assist you in laying out the capital required. If you have a bank loan, try not to increase it periodically, as the interest charged on such a loan might eventually become so burdensome that it prevents you from achieving the kind of success and financial freedom you're aiming for.

Compound Interest

It is important, just for a moment, to standstill here and consider the issue of compound interest. Interest, very simply put, is the increase in the capital amount of your loan by way of a certain percentage. But, that's not the only extent to which interest on a loan will burden you. Say, for instance, that you pay ten percent interest per year on a specific loan which the bank has granted you. You have to remember that, during the second year of that loan, you're not only paying interest on the original capital amount of the loan itself, but you're also paying interest on the interest which accrued during the first year. During the third year, you're paying *interest on interest on interest*, and so on as the years progress. This is known as the principle of compound interest and it is the reason why you can end up paying back more than twice the effective amount of the original loan, by way of interest.

Compound interest is a concept which many very successful business people still don't understand well enough, prompting them to borrow ever more money from financial institutions, such as banks. Eventually such a person becomes nothing more than a slave to the bank and all their labour and efforts are spent in an attempt to simply keep servicing the interest on their loans.

But, compound interest is not something which necessarily needs to be your enemy. You also earn interest on your investments and this is where you can use compound interest to your own benefit. Just as it is with bank loans, you can also end up earning *interest on your interest* when it comes to investments. When you start using the principle of compound interest to multiply the value of your investments exponentially, year by year, you are making this principle work in your favour, rather than allowing it to become a millstone around your neck.

The basic principle here is simple: don't allow the interest payable on capital to become a burden to you, but rather make it one of the ways in which you further your own interests. Try not to become too dependent on banks and, as mentioned before, make sure that you present your business to prospective investors in order to lure them into your circle and make them your business partners. As long as they keep receiving good dividends on their investment, they will stay by your side and become the kind of partners which will ultimately propel you to your destiny. Don't be afraid to employ the services of a good financial advisor to explain the principle of compound interest in more detail to you. Such a person will also be able to formulate a specific financial plan, which will ultimately benefit you as you grow your business. Remember that the principle of compound interest is not something which will make its effect felt overnight. It is something which grows exponentially, meaning that it might start off slowly, but one day explode to either become a source of incredible wealth, or a massive financial burden to you.

{ **Now is the Time to Create a Habit of Saving** }

Just as you did with other things, such as laying out a pattern of consistent positive thinking, you need to do the same when it comes to financial habits.

When you think about saving, you probably think of it in terms of putting some money away whenever you have extra finances which you do not intend to immediately spend on anything. This is a great way to start, but this is not saving in the true sense which is required if you want to become a FITpreneur. You need to decide on a specific percentage of your monthly income and save it every month. Perhaps you decide to start with five percent. Even though this amount may not seem to be a lot, you'll be surprised at the kind of growth you can achieve, with the influence of compound interest, if you just put away five percent of your earnings every month. The fact that you're making it a habit is also important as you are, once again, reinforcing your mind with the idea that you're working towards a specific outcome and not merely taking things as they come.

Whilst you are busy forming positive habits, such as saving and regular investment, you should also spend some time to start breaking down the negative financial habits which you may have formed over the years. Perhaps you have spent way too much money on your credit card and are already suffering from the incredibly high interest which you need to pay on the outstanding balance. While you are making a habit of putting away some money in your savings account every month, also make a habit of repaying a certain percentage of your credit card every month and stop using it for your financial expenses.

What to Invest in

When it comes to the specific nature of stocks you should invest in, you may want to consult your financial advisor and ask him to put together an investment portfolio for you. Don't invest all of your money in high-yield, high-risk investments, but also make sure that you invest in some more conservative things like gold, which may not yield an incredible increase, but is always a safe investment. Likewise, when you decide to invest your money in company shares, don't only go for new, fast-growing companies, but also take some time to invest in the so-called blue-chip companies which have proven their worth over the years.

Buy low, sell high

The above is a fairly simple principle, yet many people lose their money every day on the stock exchange because they do not follow it. Take a moment to think, for example, of something like Bitcoin. When Bitcoin started out, no one was too excited about it and most people thought it would just be a passing fad. But, as the price started to increase exponentially, more and more people started investing in Bitcoin and eventually the price skyrocketed. After some time, almost everyone bought themselves some Bitcoin and the ones who invested right towards the end lost a lot of their money when the Bitcoin price crashed. What is the lesson to be learned from this? Simple. Don't buy stocks, such as Bitcoin, when it seems to be skyrocketing in price. If you buy at this point, you are *buying high*. The secret is to *buy low*. This means that you should invest in something like Bitcoin when no one else is interested in it. Not only do you get it at a relatively low price that way, but you also minimise your risk. Unfortunately, most people believe in the unfounded wisdom of '*running with the pack*' and they will buy something like Bitcoin when the price goes up and everyone else is buying it. In doing so, they are disobeying the simple rule of *buy low, sell high*.

Diversification

Another important principle when it comes to the art of good investment is Diversification. Diversification means that you shouldn't invest all of your money in the same kind of stocks. Do not, for example, choose a lot of high-tech computer companies and invest your money in all of them. The reason for this is that, if computer stocks should crash, you will lose all of your money in one go. Make sure that you invest in a wide, diverse range of stocks, thereby minimising your risk. You may also want to take out some bonds, as this will provide an even greater degree of diversification to your investment portfolio. Once again, your financial advisor can explain these principles to you in more detail.

You will notice that we are already assuming that, at this point, you're going to make enough money to have something left over, after your savings and credit card payments, to invest in stocks. The reason for this is that we have faith in your ability to make a success and profit right from the outset. If you have taken the proper steps to lay out the foundation for your journey, then there is no reason why you shouldn't be financially profitable in your business right from the start. Some people lay out business plans which envisage a loss, for a number of years, before they will ever see a profit. Stay away from those kind of businesses. A good business is something which makes profit from day one, even if it doesn't pay off all of the loans and capital which has been invested in the business immediately. This means, very simply, that you should not buy apples at fifty pence each and sell them at forty pence each, in a misguided attempt to build a client base. Right from the outset, a fifty pence apple should be sold for at least sixty pence, so that there is an immediate profit. The example may seem simple, but it is surprising to see how many people fail to follow it, thereby making their eventual success very difficult.

Calculated financial risks

At the outset, you will have to learn how to take calculated risks. I'm not referring you to the kind of risk which a gambler takes when he bets on a hand of cards which may come out in any unpredictable way. That kind of risk is an *uncalculated risk*, or a *blind risk*. A calculated risk is a risk which may be assessed to a certain degree. For example, if you see the oil price tumbling, you may take the calculated risk of buying some shares in oil when the price is low, hoping that the price will soon go up again. This is a calculated risk. The reason why it is not a blind risk, is that there is the conventional wisdom that the oil price, eventually, has to start rising again, as it is a commodity which is required for almost every kind of commerce in the world.

Another kind of calculated risk is when you seek additional capital, by way of a bank loan for additional investors, to expand your business. Perhaps you decide to build another factory, or to open another head premises in a different town. This, also, is a calculated risk. It means that you have the kind of confidence in your business which makes it possible for you to seek expansion, even though you will have to lay out additional capital in order to achieve it.

All of your calculated risks will not always work out the way you want them to. Perhaps you take out a loan from the bank to open an additional factory and the bank decides to move up the interest rate right after you have taken out the loan. This isn't something you can control and, as hard as it may seem, it should not stop you from taking other, calculated risks in the future. On the other hand, you may also have an unexpected windfall, such as a healthy increase in your business once the second factory has been opened.

Tax

Once you start making money, you have to remember that you're also going to be liable for tax. It is simply a fact of life and you should not forget to make provision for the payment of your government taxes. Remember that there are certain ways in which you can minimise your tax liability. At this stage you should be careful to make a very clear distinction between *tax evasion* and *tax avoidance*. Tax evasion is illegal as it is a process whereby a person, or company, may seek to evade paying the taxes for which they are legally liable. If you evade your taxes you are walking down a very dangerous path which will eventually cause you to get into conflict with the powers that be. Tax avoidance, on the other hand, is perfectly legal. It is the process by which you structure your business in such a way that you pay as little taxes as possible, without breaking the law. To avoid the unnecessary payment of high taxes, you should employ a tax consultant who is an expert in the area of tax avoidance. Such a person will help you structure your business in such a way that you minimise the payment of your taxes in a legal way.

Domestic Budgeting

We have already discussed the importance of not placing all of your eggs in one basket, when it comes to investment. But you also have to do some planning when it comes to your domestic spending, in other words the kind of money which you will be applying to your home and your family life. Many people make the mistake of doing very careful planning in their business and setting up a rigid pattern of regular saving and investment there, whilst neglecting the creation of a similar structure for their domestic spending. For example, a person may have five thousand pounds a month which he can spend in any way on his house and family. If such a person has a domestic budget, he may find that he only needs to spend four thousand pounds of the five thousand, leaving him with an additional one thousand pounds to save or invest. He can do this because he has carefully budgeted and laid out his monthly domestic expenses. A person, on the other hand, who does not budget, will go ahead and spend the five thousand pounds every month, including expenditure on items which may be unnecessary. In doing so, the second person is losing out on the opportunity of using the extra thousand pounds for additional investment, or even to raise the capital investment in his business. For this reason, it is essential that you should also set up a careful structure of budgeting for your domestic expenditure.

Setting up a domestic budget is not something which you need expert help to achieve. All that is required is for you to sit down and make a list of everything you need to pay every month when it comes to your family. This will include things such as rent, electricity, car payments and food. Add to this also a healthy amount for unforeseen expenses, as these always seem to crop up. Now that you have made provisions for your monthly domestic expenditure, including an amount for unforeseen circumstances, you should be disciplined and stick with it. The temptation to spend extra on unnecessary things will always be there, but you should resist it. You may also have to educate your family to accept a greater degree of responsibility in curbing wasteful expenses.

You may want to take the time, at this point, to sit your loved ones down and explain to them that there is a very specific reason why you are taking steps to set up a domestic budget. Once they understand that your ultimate aim is to achieve the kind of wealth and financial freedom which will ultimately also benefit them, they will be far more willing to take part in domestic budgeting, as they will realise that they are working towards their own financial increase. Teach your children to accept responsibility for the pocket money you give them every month. It is never too soon for them to start learning about saving. You should teach them to set up their own little budgets to start the healthy habit of financial planning as early as possible. In doing so, you are taking the kind of steps which your parents may have neglected with you, thereby giving your children the winning edge which you may never have had as a child.

Success breeds Success

The saying that success breeds success is actually something which has its origin in ancient Indian poetry and it is very true, even in today's modern times. It refers to the principle that, once you have made a substantial amount of money, that money will turn itself into even more money with little effort. For example, if you have a hundred thousand pounds in the bank and keep saving it and gaining compound interest year-by-year, that money alone will end up owning you an amount equal to a reasonably good working salary. But that is not very dense. Once you have some money and people can see that you are successful, they are far more likely to invest in your business and may be willing to take some of their own money and help you increase your business capital. The same can also be slightly adjusted to suggest that success breeds even more success, which makes it even more applicable to our modern century.

The secret is to reach that threshold beyond which you have a substantial amount of working capital or money saved up in the bank. Once you've reached that first steppingstone, the journey becomes a lot easier as you no longer experience the consistent pressure of having to make enough just to get by. This is why it is important to set yourself some milestones as intermediary goals on your journey. You have already decided that you, ultimately, want to become a FITpreneur, but that doesn't mean that this should be your only set goal. Perhaps you should also make the first achievement on your list the accumulation of at least a hundred thousand pounds in your bank account. Then, after that, you may aim at two hundred thousand pounds and so on. Perhaps you can even reward yourself with a special holiday each time you reach one of your goals, thereby providing some additional inspiration for artwork to get to the next one. Many FITpreneurs can testify of the powerful effect that intermediary goalposts can have on the prospects of your ultimate success.

Another important practical consideration is to shop around when you are building your business. Perhaps you have decided to set up an auto repair business. You may find yourself in an industrial area where you have many prospective suppliers of all the order parts you need to carry on your business and, without really giving it a second thought, you may simply start using them as your supplies. But have you taken the time to investigate the possibility of importing these parts from a country like China? Perhaps it might be more effort and a slightly higher admin load for you to import the order parts, but you may end up getting it for fifty percent cheaper and thereby increase your profit margin significantly. Don't be satisfied with the first available deal and make the effort of shopping around to find out whether something better might be available.

CHAPTER FIVE

Building your own FITpreneur Business

Having your own fitness empire is probably a dream you have carried in your heart for a long time and it is the very reason you started reading this book. Without saying it in so many words, much of our discussion so far has been built on the implied premise that you are going to start your own fitness business. For the sake of clarity, it would be helpful to pause for a moment and more clearly elucidate this concept.

If you think that it is possible to become a FITpreneur by working for someone else in his fitness business, just consider for a moment how many of your friends and family have been working for other people all their lives, without even getting close to having their own business. If you consider the odds, you will understand that the prospects of becoming a FITpreneur by working for someone else are very small indeed, if not entirely non-existent. Forget about forming a partnership with someone else, for example at an existing gymnasium. By far the best way of becoming a fitness business owner is to have your own gym and to operate it yourself. Of course, this is much harder work than simply handing in your CV, going for a job interview and starting to work at a gym. But, in the long run, the rewards far outweigh the additional effort which it will require from you. When you start your own fitness business you not only become your own boss, you also set your own limits and you can aim as high as you like, without having to get someone else's approval first.

Remember, in setting up your own fitness business, that you are going to need the right personnel and staff members to assist you. You have already gone to great lengths to prepare a business environment where you have harnessed all of the positive energies of the universe to work in your favour. Now comes the next important step, namely hiring the right people. The first thing you should do is to make sure that you have the right trainers to work in your exercise area. You may want to start off small, but the appointment of competent managers are also absolutely essential. Not only should they be people who are highly competent in their areas of expertise, they should also be reliable and be the kind of personnel that will add a positive energy to your workout environment.

In appointing the right staff, you may incur a high level of additional expenditure, but in the long run it will be worth it. Now is the time to tighten your domestic budget and to make sure that every available penny goes into the hiring of the right personnel for your business. Remember that this is only a passing phase and that the return on your investment in competent staff will soon start reaping its own rewards.

Additional income

It would be helpful if you can also get assistance from your life partner in making their own dispensable income available for the purposes of building the business. Just think for a moment of the examples you may have seen of dual income families in your own area. Perhaps the husband drives a very low-key vehicle and doesn't dress too flashy. He works hard, spends long hours at the premises and doesn't spend his money on much else than his business. But his wife might be a different kettle of fish altogether. Perhaps she drives a very flashy sports car, wears expensive clothes and lavish perfumes. She might have her own well-paying job, yet she doesn't have her husband's sense of frugality and responsibility when it comes to spending money. Now just imagine how much quicker they would be able to grow her husband's business if the lady decided to stop having such a lavish lifestyle and to make a part of her income available for the purposes of furthering her husband's business. For a while, she may have to stop spending so much money on herself, but in the long run she will quickly get a high return on her investment in her husband's business. Within a year or two his business may quickly double in size and income and not only will his wife be able to return to her previous level of living, she may even be able to surpass it!

Having a dual income in a household can be a very powerful tool in building your own fitness business and you should be prepared to have a tough, honest discussion with your life partner to assess the prospects of combining the dual income for the purposes of growing a new business.

{ **Take time to develop your own skills** }

Despite what you may have heard, most FITpreneurs do not succeed at their very first try in business. Maybe the very first large gym they open does make them millions of pounds, but that does not necessarily mean that it was their first attempt at starting a fitness business. Many of these men and women will tell you how they often started creating small workout areas at home as children. Perhaps they worked out there with their fellow students at school. But they used this experience to set them up for ultimate success.

If you have never tried to start a business as a child, do not despair. It is never too late to try for the first time, as long as you are willing to accept failure as a part of the learning process. Through every failure, you will sharpen your skills and increase your knowledge as fitness business owner.

Delegation

One of the very important things you will need to learn as a new business owner is how to delegate. Perhaps you are a great trainer and try to do all of the training yourself. Initially, your decision may seem like a wise one, as you will do high quality training and quickly get a great reputation. But you are losing sight of the fact that such an approach might be very shortsighted. What are you going to do once your business starts growing exponentially? There will be far too much training for you to do it all by yourself and you may find yourself rushing to complete all of the work personally. Eventually, this is going to lead to a decline in your training quality and, eventually, the sterling reputation you may have built for yourself will start going down the drain. This is because you have not yet considered the importance of the principle of delegation.

From the outset, no matter how skilled you are at any particular aspect of your own fitness business, you should train others and teach them to reach the same level of expertise as you. You should appoint other trainers to share the workload and initially oversee their training to make sure that it is on a high level. Eventually, you may end up doing none of the training yourself and simply oversee your trainers in a supervisory capacity. This is the correct business model and the one you should strive towards. Many businesses reach an invisible ceiling, beyond which no growth is possible, simply because their owners never understood and implemented the correct level of delegation. If you delegate correctly, you will not only manage to shift a lot of the workload away from yourself, you'll also give others the opportunity of growing in the business. When your employees notice that you are also helping them to grow personally, they will appreciate the opportunity of working for you and this will eventually inspire them to make even greater efforts to assist you in growing your fitness business effectively.

CHAPTER SIX

Choose the best Fitness Business model

As you probably know from experience, there are various kinds of fitness business models around and only you will know which one suits your own personal skills and abilities.

One of the most important things you have to decide before you take the step of setting up your own gym or fitness business, is to decide which business model suits you the best with reference to your own special skills and abilities. You have probably given this a lot of thought already and we can assume that you know your own strengths and your own weaknesses. But bear in mind that, even if you already know which direction you want to go in with your business, there's always the opportunity to more accurately focus your efforts.

Perhaps you have decided that you want to open a large gymnasium. You have found the right investors and trainers. Perhaps fitness training is something which you have done for many years, working for someone else. Now that you are ready to start your own fitness business, it is important to make sure that you don't simply create the same kind of company that you have worked for in the past. Perhaps there are certain things which you can improve on, such as choosing a better neighbourhood, or perhaps a cheaper area to build the gym. Just because previous places you may have worked for concentrated on a specific part of the market, doesn't mean that this is something which you should also do. Take some time to consider your own experience, special abilities and training and then start a fitness business which most effectively utilises all of your own personal skills.

Education

One of the very important questions which you need to answer is whether you require any additional training yourself before you start your business. Remember that the idea of starting your own fitness business can be a very imposing and perhaps even intimidating one. You may feel as if you are not really qualified to start your own business, and therefore embark on a long process of never-ending levels of additional education. This would be a mistake. The longer you spend in the education cycle, the less time you have in the moneymaking cycle. Remember that your time is limited and you need to spend it as wisely as possible. Once an hour is wasted, you can never have it back. Getting a lot of business degrees does not guarantee that you will eventually have a successful business.

Most FITpreneurs, as mentioned before, cut their teeth on smaller fitness businesses and learn by way of trial and error, rather than spending many years at college to get impressive business degrees behind their names. When you look for the traits that are most common amongst FITpreneurs, a high level of education isn't one of them. Instead, you'll find that they are all passionate, ambitious, confident and purpose driven. Spend your time focusing your energies towards the dream which you have carried in your heart all of these years. If you really need to get additional education, try to do it on the job, perhaps through correspondence or an online course. This way you won't waste any time in the practical, hands-on development of your business skills.

Working hours

If you have always been the kind of person who worked eight hours a day, five days a week, then there is no reason for you to change this pattern once you start your own fitness business. If you delegate your work correctly, you may soon find that you have some extra time on your hands, as you will not be performing all of the labour yourself. But remember that this business has always been a dream of yours and it is probably something you will enjoy doing. Under the circumstances, continue to spend sufficient time at work and don't fall into the habit of staying at home and letting others run your company. Not only is this something which might have a negative impact on your own mental well-being, you will also risk the possibility that those who run your company will neglect it when they sense that you are not really fully committed to it. Most FITpreneurs love what they do and, in fact, spend every single available hour at work in order to develop their businesses. Of course, you should also make time for your family and make sure that you do not neglect your loved ones, but a careful balance should be struck here. You should never fall into the trap of spending too much time at the premises, or too much time at home.

Your Future Vision

When you decide exactly what kind of fitness business to embark on, you should also use your experience to make certain projections for the future. Perhaps you have been working in a gymnasium for a very long time and have a good sense of the kind of workouts which clients are demanding. Perhaps you have noticed that there is a growing demand for circuit workouts, or some other kind of exercise. Use this knowledge to make certain projections for the future and to get a sense of the best business direction to go in with your own fitness company'. If you believe that the future is in free weights, make this a part of your gym layout right from the outset. Don't try to copy the gymnasiums you may have worked in the past, but rather use your vision for the future to dictate how you set up your own fitness business.

Having a vision for the future is one of the ways you can gain an edge above the competition. This is where you can focus on the gap you have spotted in the market and set up your business in such a way that, right from the outset, you start making money in an area where none of your competitors have focused their efforts.

You may also want to consider the possibility of specializing in a certain field. If you have spent many years working as a trainer of gymnasts, you may decide that the time has come for you to open your own gym which specializes in this kind of training. Perhaps you have noticed that there is a specific need in your area for a large gym to train athletes, or even the possibility of opening several small gymnasiums to specialise in this field. Now is the time to focus your efforts, in a laser like fashion, to specialise in the exact area where you think the most money is going to be made in the future.

In deciding exactly what kind of fitness business you're going to be operating, you should also be open to considering some of the negative criticisms which people may have had of you in the past. Have some of your colleagues at work remarked that you are too focused on your own work and don't care enough about the rest of your team? Even if you don't really believe that their criticism was valid, take some time and ask yourself whether there is not a kernel of truth in what they might have said. Perhaps it isn't completely true that you don't care about the rest of your team, but you may still discover that you could spend more time coordinating your efforts with those working around you. Make this part of your planning and remind yourself that your business will only be a great success if you manage to put together a team which works well as a unit. You will be the head of that unit and you need to inspire and direct your personnel in such a way that they will deliver their best efforts towards a common goal.

Set up a business plan

The setting up of a business plan does not need to be a complicated issue. It would do you no good to set up a fifty page business plan, with step-by-step considerations of the way in which you want to start your business, if you never get working on it. It is far better to have a simple, five-step business plan, as long as you are going to take the first couple of steps as soon as possible to get your business off the ground.

In setting up a business plan, the important considerations will be the kind of capital you are going to require, the number of staff members and trainers you will need and the kind of expenses you can expect to have on a monthly basis. It would be a good idea to set up your own, simple business plan and then present it to a financial advisor who can help you refine it in greater detail. But you definitely need to plan. Once you have set up a good, solid business plan, it is important that you use some of the pointers we have already discussed, namely the enhancement of a positive energy flow in accordance with the principles of Feng Shui and Vasta.

Once you have combined your business plan with some Feng Shui and other important construction principles, you will be ready to actually start doing business. At this point, you have already decided which staff you're going to employ and you are ready to appoint the right managers to overlook certain areas of your fitness business. You have also made provision for the delegation of duties and you are confident that you have a sufficient capital layout to set up the business, as well as cover your initial monthly expenses. Now that you are ready to start training, it is important that you must set yourself certain targets. As discussed before, a good business is one which is profitable right from the start, so you should set up certain profit targets for the first couple of months doing business. If you do not reach each and every target you've set, this should not concern you too much. The importance of setting a target is not really in achieving the exact number of sales or the amount of profit you are aiming at, but rather that you are aiming at something. There is an old saying that, if you aim at nothing, you are sure to hit it. This saying is very true. If you simply start doing business and decide to see what happens, you will most probably fail. But, if you make sure that you set yourself ambitious targets you will have something to aim at and your entire staff will know what the business is trying to achieve financially.

{ **Great management is the key to a successful fitness business** }

Having already spent some time to appoint the right managers and the right trainers, you are now in a position to create the best management team possible for your business. Perhaps you decide to include the heads of certain departments, or the most important managers, on a permanent board which has weekly meetings to discuss the progress of the fitness business. You will probably be the managing director of this board and will chair the meetings. Whatever the shape of your management team eventually looks like, the important thing is that you should have such a management team. Think of your management team as the captain and stewards of a big ship. You are the captain and you must delegate the management duties to the rest of your management team in such a way that you all work together to steer the ship in the right direction. A poor management team is the kind of team which exercises so little control over their big business ship that it eventually runs aground on the beach. A great management team, on the other end, directs the business like a stable ocean liner and takes it right to its desired destination.

Sacrifices

At the outset of your fitness business, you will need to make certain sacrifices. Perhaps you spend a lot of time watching too much TV, while you can use this time to plan your business or to refine certain aspects of it. Make a decision to sacrifice some of the time you spend in front of the TV and use it to do business and financial planning. Just like everything else we have already discussed, such a sacrifice should not be done in a piecemeal fashion. You should set aside a certain amount of time, which you would otherwise have spent in front of the TV, and find a place where you can sit down and utilise this time in a disciplined way. Perhaps you want to sit in front of your laptop and start using this extra time to work out a new distribution deal for your products, or maybe you want to use it to refine your future vision for the business. Whatever you decide to do during this period, make sure that you use the time as wisely as possible. You will soon find that your sacrifice will yield great results in practice.

You may also want to sacrifice some unnecessary expenses you have been incurring in the past. Perhaps you have spent too much money on your hobby, such as golf. Instead of buying new golf clubs or new golfing outfits, save that money and invest it in your business. Remember that this is just a temporary measure and that all of these sacrifices will eventually yield great rewards for you. One of the most important things about a sacrifice is the fact that it also inspires you to work harder at your business. When you're working at the premises, you will know that you have given up some of your favourite TV programs, or sacrificed the possible purchase of a really great set of golf clubs, and this will inspire you to work even harder to make your sacrifices worth it.

CHAPTER SEVEN

Know your Direction

You know that you want your own fitness empire and you know this is your true passion in life.

When you get to this part of the book, I trust that you have followed all the steps outlined in the previous chapters. You have set up your fitness business, according to a careful business plan, and it is now harnessing all of the positive energies around you to make it a smooth operation. You have also chosen the kind of fitness business which will most effectively complement your own specific skills and character. You have a great management team in place and they are doing a great job of steering your business in the right direction, with you at the helm.

Now it is important for you to stay on course. You may encounter some unforeseen difficulties and unexpected obstacles, especially if this is your first business. If you are not one hundred percent certain of the direction in which you want to go, you may be tempted to change some fundamental aspects of your business at the first sign of trouble or difficulty. Perhaps you have started your own large gym and decided to specialise in training athletes, yet you don't seem to find enough clients in the first couple of weeks to make your fitness business profitable. The temptation might be there for you to start branching out into other areas, despite the fact that you have designed your entire fitness business to be set up for training athletes. Don't be misled into changing your direction so quickly! Stick with your original plan and the direction that you have chosen. Remind yourself that you have spent a lot of time projecting your vision of the future onto your own personal business plan and that none of this has been created on the spur of the moment. You have carefully chosen the area where you want to do your business and you shouldn't change it just because things might take some time to get started. If you know your direction and have faith in the fact that you have chosen it well, you should stay on course and not be so quick to panic when you face your first obstacles.

Continue to visualise your success

I trust that, at this stage, you are running your fitness business in such a way that you are striving towards the achievement of certain targets. Perhaps you've decided that you want to make at least fifty thousand pounds profit in your first year. You need to really believe in the direction you have chosen and keep visualising the achievement of your targets. Even if business is slow during the first couple of months, keep visualising the moment when you will ultimately achieve the target you have set. Don't ever settle for a different vision than the one you originally had in your mind. Remember to keep programming your mind, with self-hypnosis and Trataka, to truly believe and achieve your dreams.

You should take some time to make sure that your visualisation takes on a concrete form in your business. For example, if you have visualised the kind of business premises which would catch the eye of people walking by on the street, then you should make sure that your business lives up to your visualisation. Even if it costs you a little bit extra, make sure that you create a business environment which very closely matches the original visualisation you had in your mind when you started setting up the business. Of course, you may find that you need to make small adjustments to some parts of your original vision. Perhaps you visualised a gym on the ground floor of a building, but only manage to find premises on a second floor somewhere. Even though this may not exactly match the original vision you had in your mind for your business premises, you can still make sure that the inside of your exercise area stays close to your original vision. The important thing to remember is that you should stick as closely as possible to your original visualisation, and not compromise simply because a different route may seem to be easier.

In the final analysis, your visualisation should never amount to anything less than the dream you have always carried in your heart for your own business. That dream, or vision, that you have always had is the secret to your ultimate success. As long as you keep visualising the successful materialisation of your vision, you will always stay on track and maintain your direction towards your ultimate goal of becoming a FITpreneur.

CHAPTER EIGHT

Formulate a Plan of Action

Even if your ultimate aim is simply to have a successful gym where star athletes come to work out, you will still need a detailed plan to make this vision a reality. It won't be as simple as just finding premises and buying some exercise equipment, as there are already too many fitness businesses around which have nothing more than this to offer their clients.

Bearing in mind the kind of careful planning you have already undertaken when setting up your fitness business, and maximising your use of the universe's positive energy, it is clear that a definite plan of action is key to becoming a FITpreneur.

You have probably already decided which line of fitness training you're going to embark upon and you also have the right trainers, business premises and investors lined up. But this doesn't necessarily mean that you have the right plan of action. A plan of action is something more than simply a business plan; it is the battle plan which you have to formulate before you start doing business. A business plan is the practical blueprint for the way you are going to run your business. For example, this will include the capital layout, the kind of personnel you're going to employ and the kind of training which will be the main focus of your fitness business. A plan of action is more of a visionary idea than the actual business plan. In formulating a plan of action, you will set certain goals and you will aim at certain targets. For example, you may set out a plan of action in which you aim to get your first hundred clients within two years and, in more clearly defining the specifics of your plan of action, you might have smaller targets leading up to that one big target. You might also have a vision of expansion and the possibility of opening up more gymnasiums in order to make your fitness business grow. The plan of action is the midway point between your concrete business plan and the dreams you had as a child.

In formulating a plan of action, it is very important that you keep doing the exercises of self-hypnosis and positive reinforcement of your ideals and concrete beliefs. You have to make sure that you set aside some time every day to meditate on a plan of action and make it a part of your belief system. Go through all of the exercises we've already touched upon in this book and use them to make your plan of action the structure according to which your subconscious mind projects your plans for the future into concrete reality.

{ ## You should have short-term, midterm and long-term goals }

In formulating your plan of action it might be helpful to have short-term, midterm and long-term goals. For example, your short-term goal might be to get two hundred clients, whereas your midterm goal might be to get five hundred clients in five years. You may not know exactly when you will reach your ultimate goal, but your long-term goal should also form a part of your plan of action.

Try to at least envision the rough period within which your entire plan of action will come into fruition. Even if you can get no closer than defining it as a period of ten years, this is still better than having an undefined period of time within which you aim to fully realise your plan of action. The reason for this is that you don't want your ultimate goal to become something of a fantasy in your mind. If you allow yourself an indefinite period within which to ultimately achieve all of your aims, you might just fall into the habit of thinking of your aims as fantasies or dreams, and not necessarily as things which will ever materialize in practice. It is absolutely essential that your plan of action includes certain time periods and also an ultimate period within which all of it needs to materialize. In laying down such guidelines you are making sure that your mind stays alert and active in formulating practical applications which will ultimately enable you to make your dreams a reality within a certain period of time.

Don't fall for Myths

It is important that you stay realistic and rational in formulating a plan of action. Some people have mythical beliefs about the way in which others become FITpreneurs. For example, they might believe that the only way to really become a fitness business owner is to be lucky. How often have you heard friends and family refer to someone else's success as 'pure luck'. They might even call it 'pure, dumb luck'. The reason people say this is because it takes the pressure off of themselves to try and achieve the same thing. After all, if all of those FITpreneurs only became so successful because they were lucky, then luck might strike at any moment and make all of your friends and family successful too. If luck is the true determining factor in whether you become successful or not, then you have absolutely no responsibility to try and reach your goals. You just have to live your life and hope that luck may also knock on your door one day. The truth of it is, of course, that most FITpreneurs plan their success very carefully. Even though their ultimate, meteoric rise to success may seem to come overnight, if you go back and look at their lives you will see that they've spent many years, and perhaps even decades, to plan their ultimate success. A famous man once remarked, *"It took me twenty years to become an overnight success!"*

Becoming a fitness business owner is not just luck. Even though some people may be more fortunate than others in the world of business, eventually it is something which comes down to planning.

Another myth which you may have heard is that you can only become successful through persistent, hard work. I'm not trying to suggest that hard work does not make up an essential part of any plan of action to become a FITpreneur, but hard work alone will not do it for you. If hard work was the key to wealth, then why aren't more of your friends and family rich, when they have been working hard in their jobs all of their lives? It's not necessarily just a question of how hard you work, but also how smart you work. One thing which people forget when they so glibly suggest that hard work is the key towards becoming successful, is that their hard work may be spent exclusively for the benefits of making someone else successful. They work at a company where they do splendid work, but they never share in any of the profits of that company. Such a person might work extremely hard, yet they get the same salary every month, regardless of how excellent their work was during that specific month. The key to becoming successful is to see a connection between your excellence and the money you earn for your labour.

Another popular myth is that there is a secret formula which will guarantee the achievement of success, if only you can find it. It's almost as if people think that there is a magic elixir which, once consumed, will give them the magical ability to become successful overnight. You may even have picked up this book with the thought that it will contain that magic formula. That magic formula, unfortunately, does not exist, yet there is indeed a secret to becoming successful and that's what this book is all about. But remember that the secret is not to be found somewhere out there. The secret is inside you! You see, those dreams and ideals which you have always had are the ultimate keys to your success. They've been placed inside you by the wisdom of the universe and the benevolence of Providence. All you need to do is look inside yourself, identify those dreams and ideals and formulate a plan of action to make them a concrete reality.

Everything comes down to a plan of action. Once you understand that you have the secret keys to your own success inside you, you won't mind going through all of the exercises in this book and reconditioning your mind to become a powerful tool which will ultimately help you create your own fitness business. Don't listen to myths and don't lend your ears to people who have had no great financial success in their own lives. If a man has had four businesses and all of them have gone bankrupt, would you go to him for financial advice? No, of course not. The same goes for all of those people who might come to you with their clever stories and advice regarding the acquisition of wealth. Just look at their lives and ask yourself whether their own advice has been of any great benefit to them. If they are poor and unsuccessful, you would be foolish to even consider their advice. Take some time to look at people who have made it big in business and you will find, as we have mentioned before in this book, that they all have certain things in common. They save, they are visionaries, they work for themselves. Consider all of these ingredients and make them a part of your plan of action.

CHAPTER NINE

Minimise your Expenses

It is time now to return to a thought which we have already discussed earlier. Frugality. One of the most common traits which all businessmen and women share is frugality. They all save. But this does not necessarily mean they take each penny they earn and put it in the bank. Even though that kind of saving is also important, the true meaning of frugality is to actually cut back on unnecessary expenses.

There is no point in setting up a careful business plan and a plan of action without also including therein the idea of cutting back on your expenses. The first place where you will be able to save is in your domestic expenditure. We've already discussed the possibility of getting your spouse to contribute a part of their income to the capital layout of your business. But, even if your spouse does not work, they can still make a positive contribution towards the saving of domestic expenditure. For example, they can start cutting back on extravagant dinners and expensive toys for the children. Even though this may create a little bit of tension at first, you should sit down with your entire family and explain to them that all of you will reap the benefits eventually when your business becomes a great financial success.

One of the most important places where you can save on domestic expenditure is in car payments. Do you own a car which is unnecessarily luxurious? It is never too late to sell it and buy yourself a cheaper car. Remember that this is only a temporary measure and that you can always upgrade again when your business comes off the ground. You will find that you can save enormous amounts of money every month if you just cut down on excessive car payments and insurance.

Once you have taken all the steps to minimise unnecessary domestic expenditure, you also have to do the same thing in your business. When your business is up and running you will find that, in many cases, you learn to be more efficient as you go along. Perhaps you started off with one supplier who supplies you with raw materials for manufacturing purposes and, as you learn more about the marketplace, you discover that your supplier is actually very expensive. Don't fall into the trap of simply staying with that supplier because it is slightly uncomfortable to set up new supply routes with other, less expensive suppliers. Comfortable is not always correct and you should minimise your expenditures in every way possible, especially at the outset of your business.

Another place where you may be able to save on unnecessary expenditure is staff. Of course, you don't want to end up in a position where you have to fire people, so the best way of making sure that you don't incur unnecessary expenditure in the payment of your employees is to plan the appointment of your staff very carefully. It is better to start off with a small number of employees and gradually increase it, rather than hiring too many people and then discovering that you do not need all of them. A careful balance has to be struck here. Remember that it is important to delegate, as we've already discussed in an earlier chapter. You cannot take on all of the work personally, but you also do not want to hire so many people that they sit around all day without anything to do. Start off with a small, reliable number of employees and be open to the prospect of gradually increasing this number as the need arises and the business grows.

Another area where you can save on business expenditure is premises and gym equipment. There is no point in buying all of the latest exercise equipment for your gym when the business has not really grown to a point yet where all of this equipment is essential. As the business grows and you appoint more trainers and staff to take care of clients, you can always buy more exercise equipment. Spend your business capital wisely and try to keep some of it in reserve.

{ ## Saving on expenditure could be
the difference between success and failure }

Have you ever wondered why some people earn extremely high wages, yet they never seem to have enough? Look at some of your friends. They might be doctors, lawyers or engineers, yet they are always in the red and the never have enough money to pay all of their bills. The reason for this is that they have never learned the secret of cutting back on unnecessary expenditure. Perhaps they drive cars that are way too expensive and they eat out at restaurants too often. Their children insist on having all of the latest toys and gadgets, whilst the parents also spoil themselves with things which they cannot really afford. This soon becomes a vicious cycle, as these people often have to go to the bank and take out loans to sustain their lavish lifestyles. Soon the credit card is overdrawn and their lives become a mad cycle of simply trying to pay the interest and arrears. Don't make the same mistake as these people. It is essential that you cut back on all of your unnecessary expenses and make sure that a maximum amount of capital remains available to grow your fitness business during the early stages of its development.

CHAPTER TEN

Being a FITpreneur will take you to your Dreams!

Just think for a second how that heading makes you feel – *Being a FITpreneur will take you to your Dreams*. You may have heard so many negative things about the fitness industry that you think it is impossible for anyone to actually succeed in it. Unfortunately, many people say negative things about business opportunities, mostly because they don't have the courage to try it for themselves. It's almost a knee-jerk reaction to the fact that they wished they could have their own business, yet seem unable of finding a way to make their own dreams come true. In direct response to their disappointment, they start saying negative things about business opportunities and you may even have made some of those negative statements a part of your own personal beliefs.

You may have heard people say that '*Money is the root of all evil*'. This is actually a misquotation from the Bible, where it is written that "*The love of money is the root of all evil.*" Regardless of your personal faith and religion, you should never fall into the trap of believing the misquotation. Money, regardless of your personal religion, is not evil. In fact, just take a moment and think about all of the positive things you'll be able to do once you have wealth.

The most important thing you will be able to do is expand your own fitness business to better serve your customers and attend to their needs.

You would also be able to build a shelter for the homeless, give money to charities and buy food for those are hungry. Do all of these things you could do with money sound evil to you? Of course not! It is only when you have true wealth that you're actually in a position to make the world a better place and, under such circumstances, money can actually be a force for good in the world.

The reason why we have to stand still for a moment and consider the true nature of money, is because it has been so poorly represented as a concept in the past. Historically, people have often thought about money as a means of oppressing the poor and overpowering those who do not have a voice. Perhaps money has been abused by certain people, yet this can never make money itself an evil force. People are evil, money is not. It is very important that you start thinking of money in positive terms. If money has certain negative connotations for you, those negative connotations will eventually become negative energies which will repel the right kind of people and opportunities from you. You need to make it part of your daily meditation and self hypnosis to welcome money into your life. You may choose to say something like, "Money and wealth, I welcome you into my life."

At first, it may seem strange to you to start thinking of money as a positive force of good in your life, but it is absolutely essential that you take this step. Once again, you may be suffering from the belief in myths which have been created by those who have lived their entire lives in poverty. Once you start thinking of money as your enemy, you will not take the appropriate steps to make more of it. It is unfortunately a fact of life that some people have such a negative view of money that they repel financial success from their lives.

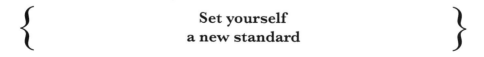

{ **Set yourself a new standard** }

What are the limitations with which you grew up? Perhaps you grew up in a nice suburb and never really suffered from poverty. You might have had some good friends in that neighbourhood and spent most of your youth hanging out with them. All of this might seem to have been positive, yet it isn't necessarily so. Many people fall into the trap of looking at the way they grew up and then formulate their own views of success according to the standards they experienced as children. Just because your parents had a comfortable life and never really suffered any lack, that doesn't mean they could not have achieved more. If you make the mistake of looking at your past as your only point of reference, you may end up falling well short of the destiny that the universe has in store for you!

Have you ever considered the fact that most successful people eventually have children who also become successful? Don't make the mistake of simply ascribing this to the fact that they inherit wealth from their parents. To a certain extent it is true that successful people leave some of their wealth to their children, yet it is not the only explanation for the fact that their entire bloodline often remain successful financially. The truth of it is that the children of successful parents formulate higher standards to aspire to. For example, if a child grows up with a father who owns a company, that child is not very likely to go and work as a mere employee in someone else's company. They are much more likely to try and start their own company one day, alternatively carry on the work that their own father did in his company. The reason for this is simple, namely that such a child sets higher ideals for himself. Conversely, if a child grows up in a family where both parents work for some company, they are likely to start thinking of this as the norm. Such children often end up also working for companies their entire lives, without ever acquiring any true wealth.

Remember that we are not talking about aspiring to a lavish, extravagant lifestyle here. When children see their parents wasting money, they are likely to do the same one day and this is most definitely not something which will help them along the way to acquiring true financial wealth. The kind of higher standards which the children of successful parents set for themselves have to do with the fact that they strive to a higher excellence and a higher set of goals for themselves. This does not necessarily involve the unnecessary expenditure of money on extravagant things such as cars, yachts and mansions. It simply refers to the fact that someone with higher ideals *think of themselves differently*. They don't see themselves as employees in someone else's company, but rather as people who were destined to have their own companies one day.

It all comes back to the way you perceive your place in the world. Unfortunately you may suffer from certain myths and misconceptions about financial wealth which have been installed in your mind by your own parents. They may have meant well, yet it is possible that those things which they taught you as a young child have actually become limitations on your future. If your parents only ever encouraged you to work for other people, they may have missed the possibility of giving you a higher vision for your future. Now is the time to shake off those beliefs and to break yourself free from the shackles which have kept you imprisoned all of these years! It is not necessary to disrespect your parents in order to leave behind certain incorrect instructions which they have given you over the years. You can still love your parents, yet find a way of setting your sights on higher ideals than those your parents had for you.

Money can buy excellence

One of the most important things to remember when you consider the true nature of money, is that it has the power of buying excellence. We've already discussed the fact that money holds the possibility of establishing good things in the world, such as charities and contributions towards the alleviation of poverty. But there is another very important thing which money can buy, namely excellence. I am referring here to the possibility of hiring the best minds to become a part of your business. When you start out you may not have the kind of capital layout required to hire the best trainers and equipment for your gymnasium. But, as you become more successful, you may start seeing the possibility of employing more excellent trainers and buy new equipment to take your business to the next level. This is one of the best things you can do with your money, as it will enable you to exponentially grow the profitability of your fitness business. Remember that you might have your own specific field of expertise, whilst others can come into your business and provide a totally different point of view and new, constructive approach.

{ **Make sure that your appearance tells people who you are** }

We have spent considerable time in previous chapters discussing the necessity of saving on unnecessary expenditure. It is absolutely essential that you stop wasting money on domestic luxuries which you can ill afford. In the same vein, you should not spend too much money, at the outset of your business, on unnecessary training equipment and other luxuries. But one area where you should never hold back is personal appearance.

It is not necessary to buy yourself a different suit for every day of the week, but it is essential that you have at least one or two outfits which you can wear when meeting with important clients or prospective investors. Even if you have a construction business, it is essential that you buy yourself at least one neat suit which you can wear to these occasions. People simply take a well-dressed person more seriously than a guy who shows up in dirty overalls and muddy boots. Make sure that you spend some time looking at FITpreneurs and the way they dress. Even if they do not spend thousands on the latest fashions, they always dress neatly, especially for important business meetings.

Dressing the part is not the only aspect of your appearance which you need to attend to if you wish to become successful. The way you project yourself and the way you speak are also very important. Seldom will you see a FITpreneur walking around and shouting at his trainers or staff in the gym. Successful people almost always have a strong, reserved way in which they project themselves and they speak with authority, rather than volume. Perhaps you grew up with the idea that you need to shout if you want people to listen, but that would be a mistake in the world of business. Learn to speak with authority and confidence, rather than raising your voice when you try to put your point across, especially in important business meetings.

When you have your board meetings, make sure that you give everyone a chance to speak, yet also project confidence and leadership when it is your turn to address the meeting. If you have followed all of the important Feng Shui principles we discussed in earlier chapters, your boardroom will probably have a round table for meetings, eliminating the idea that people are opposing each other during board meetings. This will already make for more constructive and healthy meetings and you should supplement this advantage by providing strong leadership during such discussions.

Opportunities

You may look at some of the people who have their own fitness empires and wonder what exactly the secret is that enables them to get all of the wonderful opportunities that keep coming their way. These are the kind of people your friends might look at and call them 'lucky'. But they don't get all of those opportunities because they're lucky. Those opportunities come their way because they have a positive, confident demeanour about them. When a person looks as if he is already successful by reason of the way he dresses and speaks, people tend to be more likely to refer important business his way. Because of his confident demeanour, others are more likely to open the doors for him and provide such a person with great business opportunities. The secret is in the way you project your positive energies to those around you. You should become a conduit for the positive energies of the universe and allow them to flow through you in such a way that others look at you and consider you worthy of the best opportunities.

The more you start paying attention to your dress code and general demeanour, the more you will start projecting positive energies to those around you and their confidence in you as a business leader will keep growing. It all starts with the hours of meditation and self-hypnosis you put in at home, during which you reinforce your subconscious mind with positive thoughts. Eventually, those positive thoughts must find a way to the outside world and you need to project them in such a way that people attach credibility to what you say. The best way to achieve that credibility is to look and sound successful.

It isn't necessary for you to be the best speaker or the most eloquent orator to achieve what we are discussing here. Projecting a positive image when you speak has much more to do with the confident tone of your voice than with the ability to use impressive words. It may feel strange at first when you force yourself to speak in a more confident, deliberate way, but it will soon become a habit and once it has become a normal part of your business personality, you will be astounded at the extra level of confidence it will inspire in the people around you. They will start looking at you as a leader and will be far more willing to open the right doors for you and send the best opportunities your way. Likewise, you might be surprised at what a difference it will make if you start dressing properly for important meetings. Where others may have looked at you with scepticism and doubt in the past, you might soon discover a brand new level of confidence and willingness to listen to your ideas. You will also find it much easier to convince new investors to lay their money down and invest in your plans.

Ultimately, the greatest edge you can give yourself above your competitors is simply to create a better visual impression than they do. In a cutthroat marketplace where the fitness business is an arena of tough competition, you will need every inch of advantage you can get over your competition and one of the most effective ways of establishing that advantage is to create a more excellent visual image they do. When your business proposal and the business proposal of a competitor look very similar on paper, your personal appearance might just tip the scales in your favour and land you a contract which you might otherwise have lost!

CHAPTER ELEVEN

Live your Passion

The most important thing you need to remember after reading this book is that your greatest passion is also your greatest source of possible wealth. That is why you should become a FITpreneur and live your passion without fear! It would do you no good to follow all of the exercises and principles laid out in the previous chapters if you fail to understand this one, fundamental truth.

Your greatest passion is fitness and all things related to it; you first dreamed about it when you were a young child. It may also be something which developed gradually as you made your way through your professional career. Perhaps you are a trainer who has spent twenty years working in someone else's gym. During this time, however, you may have developed a special knowledge and skill for training weight lifters, or perhaps you learned how to train athletes. You will know your greatest passion as the thing you spend most of your time thinking about when you are at work. It is that perfect picture which you carry in your mind of the kind of job you would like to do; the thing which excites you more than anything else.

Once you have identified your true passion in the fitness business, you are in a position to start moving towards it. Follow the patterns and suggestions in this book and start reprogramming your mind so that it becomes a powerful tool which will ultimately enable you to make your greatest passion your source of personal wealth. Do not allow anyone to talk you out of your vision once you have established it. Allow your passion and your ideals to carry you through the tough times and to see you through the disappointment which temporary failures may bring about in your life.

Remember that you should make sure to choose the right people as trainers and staff and that they should also be the kind of people who will be team players. If you are surrounded by people who support you and your vision, the tough times won't seem quite that hard and each victory will be even sweeter. Try to find people who share your passion and who will also consider the kind of business you are involved in as something which really satisfies them personally. The best employee is an employee who feels naturally attracted to the same kind of ideals that you do.

{ ## It isn't hard to make sacrifices for your true passion }

The reason why so many people find it hard to make sacrifices whenever they strive towards the attainment of a new ideal in their life, is because they are not driven by their passion. For example, a person may realise that they need to save money in order to afford gym membership fees. However, no matter how hard they may try, they never seem to be able to cut back on their unnecessary expenses and that gym membership never becomes a reality. The reason for this is that they probably do not really have a great passion for the idea of joining the gym in the first place. Perhaps they're only thinking of getting a gym membership because someone at work remarked that they are overweight, or perhaps their spouse is nagging them to join the gym. Because it is not their true passion, it is hard for them to make the sacrifices to attain it. But, if a person really wants to join the gym because they have a personal interest in it they won't mind making sacrifices towards the achievement of that ideal. Suddenly it isn't that hard to stop eating out at the restaurant twice a week, because you know you're going to need that money for your gym membership, which will ultimately enable you to exercise and get the body you have always dreamed of. The same principle applies to business. If you have really chosen the business that speaks to your own personal passion, it is not that hard to make personal sacrifices and cut back on expenditure to make the business a success.

Family

Despite the fact that you may have a personal passion for your business, it isn't always necessarily the same with your family. Your children may have different passions and other things which they truly want in life. For them, the idea of saving money so that your business can become a great success doesn't speak to their personal passion. You will have to take the time to explain to them that any cut back on unnecessary expenditure will ultimately also be to their own benefit. If your children really want to have new bicycles, explain to them that you will buy them those bicycles as soon as the business takes off. Now you are not only giving them something to look forward to, you're also making sure that your own family becomes a part of your team. There is nothing worse than a person who works hard at the office and tries his best for his family, only to come home and discover that they are unhappy because he works such long hours. When everyone shares the same vision and the same ideals, it is much easier for your family to become a part of the passionate strive towards your ideal of becoming a FITpreneur.

A healthy lifestyle

A healthy lifestyle is important for more than one reason. Firstly, if you really want to put in the kind of hard work and long hours which will be required for you to make a success of your fitness business, it is absolutely essential that you should be in good health. You should cut back on your consumption of alcohol and try to eliminate fatty foods. A good exercise regimen will also do a lot to stimulate your body and mind. Keep doing your mental exercises by applying self-hypnosis and positive reinforcement of your business ideals.

Another reason why good health is important is that it will improve your countenance and help you to maintain the kind of personal appearance which will attract clients to your gym or business. Athletes are more likely to want to work out at your gym if you look like a great athlete yourself!

All of the above reasons are important, but the most important reason why you need to have a healthy lifestyle is so that you will live long enough to enjoy the fruits of your labour. It would do you no good to follow all of the presets in this book and to ultimately attain success and become a FITpreneur, only to lose your life or health before you can actually enjoy your success.

A healthy lifestyle is something which an entire family can cultivate together. It isn't necessary for you to do heavy exercises with your family. All you need to do is go for long walks, eat healthy and perhaps play outside in the garden every now and then. Being healthy is a mindset which needs to be cultivated. If you and your family can cultivate the sort of healthy lifestyle and mindset which will prevent you from unnecessary visits to the doctor and expensive hospital bills, all of that money can be reinvested in the business and help you to achieve your ultimate goal of becoming a FITpreneur even quicker.

Use your existing assets

In striving towards the attainment of your passions and ideals it is important that you should not lose sight of the fact that your existing assets should be maintained. It would be senseless to have a passionate vision for the future and chase after it, only to discover that you have neglected the solid foundation of your existing financial assets, such as your house or long-term investments. This means that you should make sure your bond payments stay up-to-date, check the stock market regularly to make sure that your investments are producing a good yield. This is in addition to regular appointments with your financial advisor to discuss the possibility of upgrading and improving your investment portfolio. Existing assets may be used to raise bank loans, as well as further investments, and therefore they are an important way of keeping firm ground beneath your feet as you make your way towards the top.

Cultivate a Passionate Character

You should spend some time meditating on the following aspects which are common traits shared by most FITpreneurs. Not all of these things need to be an explicit part of your business plan or plan of action, but they should all form the passionate considerations which contribute towards your vision for success.

Financial independence

It almost goes without saying that all FITpreneurs eventually become financially independent. For this reason, you should strive towards a place in the future where you are not dependent on banks and financial institutions to provide you with business capital or money for your living expenses. Eliminate all credit cards and repay all of your loans as soon as possible. The greatest way of providing for you and your family is to eventually live off the profits of your business and the yield of your investment portfolio. Once you arrive at the place where you have a million in the bank and also enough investments, spread over a wide spectrum to eliminate unnecessary risk, you can truly say that you have arrived in the place of financial independence. Make this kind of independence a true passion and ideal.

Financial literacy

Most FITpreneurs are financially literate. Financial literacy is simply a concept which denotes the ability to make informed financial decisions. When you truly form an understanding of the driving forces behind your business and its profitability, you are said to have financial literacy about the mechanics of your business operation. Similarly, when you get to a place where you understand how the market works and where your investment portfolio yields the best results, you have arrived at the point of financial literacy regarding the stock market and your specific investments. It isn't necessary for you to have a degree in finances to attain this kind of literacy. At the outset you should make use of the services of a financial advisor or someone who will be able to teach you the basics of the financial considerations which will ultimately determine your success or failure in your chosen line of business.

Savings and investment

All successful FITpreneurs understand the importance of saving and prudent investment. It would be no good to attain a high level of financial literacy and understand the stock market so well that you can predict where the best profits can be made, if you do not also understand the importance of saving. By saving up money you ultimately enable yourself to make the kind of investments which will yield great results. Do not get into the habit of leveraging. Leveraging, simply put, means to borrow money for the purposes of investment, on the hopes that your investment will yield enough profit for you to repay the loan. This, in essence, is nothing more and nothing less than gambling. The best way to invest is to save up your money and invest it once you have enough to do so.

Avoid extravagance

It has been mentioned before, but it bears repetition. All successful business owners share the common trait of frugality and it is something which you simply have to learn. Having the mindset of eliminating unnecessary expenditure is indispensable if you're ever going to become a FITpreneur. You have to create the kind of self-discipline and discipline in your family members which will make this second nature. Saving and eliminating wasteful expenses isn't something which you should even think about and it should become such a natural part of your ordinary lifestyle that it eventually doesn't feel like a sacrifice at all. Make it your passion to focus on your ideals and to sacrifice luxuries where necessary.

Home ownership

Most successful businessmen own their own homes. This may seem like a rather simple observation, yet it is not. It is acceptable to rent a place for as long as you're still struggling to get your business off the ground, but once you make enough money to afford it you should buy your own place. There is nothing worse than simply pouring your hard earned cash down the bottomless well of someone else's bond repayments, by renting their place. Once you own your own home, you can also use it as collateral for raising further capital. Apart from the financial considerations, there is also an added sense of achievement and stability which you will experience once you own your own home and therefore you should make this a part of your long-term vision and passion.

Work for yourself

Your prospects of becoming a FITpreneur by working for someone else are much lower than when you work for yourself. Not only do you have better prospects of making your dreams a reality if you have your own fitness business, you will also be in a position to truly make your real passion a part of your future vision. If you know that all of your efforts are for your own account, you will be ready to work hard and tirelessly. It may not be possible for you to leave your current job immediately, but that doesn't mean that you cannot already start taking the preliminary steps of planning to have your own fitness business one day. Start saving, start doing the exercises of self-hypnosis and positive reinforcement of your subconscious mind. If you do the preliminary preparations properly, you will be in a much better position to make your business a success once you finally get to the place where you can leave your current employment and focus exclusively on getting your own business off the ground.

Responsibility

It goes without saying that, once you have your own fitness business, you are the person in charge and the person responsible for your own success or failure. At first this may seem like an additional burden and something which may initially just contribute to increasing your stress levels, but you will soon discover that it is far better to be the captain of your own ship than merely a passenger on someone else's vessel. All FITpreneurs accept responsibility for the outcomes of their actions and you should be the same. This doesn't mean that you should become so conservative in your way of thinking that you lose the ability of taking a healthy risk. Rather, the responsibility of having your own business should be something which inspires you to look at all the angles and to consider all of the possible outcomes before taking the risk of prudent investment and business expansion.

Once you understand each one of the above concepts, you will need to spend some time meditating on them and making them a part of your future vision. They also need to become your permanent passion, in other words you must get to a place where none of these ideas seem like a great effort to you. Make sure that you formulate a mental strategy which will enable you to make each one of these concepts a normal part of your daily thought process. Feel free to go back and revisit some of the previous chapters in this book, in order to better familiarise yourself with the strategies and methods used to reinforce your subconscious mind with the principles outlined above.

Finding your true passion in the fitness field, may require more work than you anticipated, but it will be worth every single minute you spend on it. To find your true fitness passion and make it a concrete reality, you will need to structure your way of thinking in such a way that each passionate impulse eventually becomes a driving force towards the materialisation of your ultimate vision.

Remember that there is only so much planning you can do before you take the first step. If you are really passionate about having your own fitness business, you shouldn't spend too much time in the planning phases, as this might ultimately become a way of permanently postponing your actions. It is much easier to change direction once you have started moving, than it is when you are stationary. Even a big ship is steered far more easily once it is in motion.

Mentorship

In following your true passion you may find great assistance from the identification of a specific mentor who may be able to assist you, either personally or just spiritually, in forming the kind of faith in your vision that will ultimately be required for you to make it a concrete reality. For example, if you want to start your own gym, it would be good for you to speak to someone who has successfully set up such a gymnasium. He might not be willing to give away all of his secrets, as you will ultimately become one of his competitors in the marketplace, but you will be surprised to discover how readily people will be willing to mentor you, as long as you approach them in a spirit of humility and admiration. Especially if you share the same kind of passion with your mentor, there should be an immediate feeling of kinship between the two of you and this can become a great source of strength on your way to raising up your own fitness business.

In the event that you have a specific fitness business idea which is so revolutionary that no one else has ever done it before you, it may be impossible for you to find the kind of mentor discussed above. But, even though there may not be anyone who has previous experience in the kind of business which you envision, you will always be able to find people who can inspire you with the faith and passion they exhibit in creating their own business. Even if the best mentorship you can find is simply by reading a book about someone who overcame many obstacles in setting up their own fitness empire, then read that book. Perhaps you decide that the book you're reading right now is the best mentor for you and that you want to revisit these pages as often as possible, to keep reinvigorating your spirit with the hope and passion which speaks from the words contained in this book. Whatever you decide, make sure that you have some source of support and ultimate inspiration which can help you through those dark hours when things become tough.

If you have a family, you should keep them informed of the progress of your business and make sure that they all are supportive of your vision. If you don't have a family, you won't have that additional source of support, but the benefit you have above a family owner is that you don't have additional expenses and you will be able to spend much more of your free time on the development of your business. Once your fitness business has become successful, you will have enough time to find the right partner with whom to start a family, so don't ever feel as if you have a deficit by reason of the fact that you may still be single.

CHAPTER TWELVE

Final Thoughts and Advice

The time has come for you to now take some kind of concrete action. You already know that you are passionate about the fitness business and that you want to create your own fitness empire.

Once you've finished reading this book you should spend some time thinking about its contents and, if necessary, revisit some of the chapters to refresh the contents in your memory. Then you should immediately spring into action. Get a piece of paper, or open up a document on your laptop and start writing down your thoughts. At first, the sentences you write may seem unstructured and directionless, but you will soon discover that there is great benefit to be gained from making your thoughts concrete in this way. As long as your vision remains something which only swirls around in your subconscious mind, it will never get structure. Once you start writing or typing out your vision you will discover that it starts taking shape in such a way that you can ultimately use it to compose a concrete business plan and plan of action. Remember that you are starting a brand-new journey and that the first couple of steps will probably be the hardest. But, if you are consistent in your efforts, you will soon discover that your mind will start operating in a brand-new way. You will discover that your subconscious mind will become a powerful tool and your thoughts will ultimately provide you with strategies and structures to enable the materialisation of your vision.

{ **Always keep your Ultimate Vision in Mind** }

Make sure that your ultimate goal of becoming a FITpreneur remains your primary focus. If you're truly serious about making it a reality, you will push everything else onto the sidelines and not allow people, thoughts or concerns to change your direction. Don't allow your friends to get you involved in meaningless activities, such as watching sports and going clubbing at night. Teach yourself to be more disciplined and force your mind to accept the fact that your patience, dreams and visions for the future are not mere fantasies. Be prepared to make sacrifices and keep reinforcing your mind with the understanding that you already have everything within you that is needed for you to become a FITpreneur. If you're still working for someone else, make sure that you don't spend every waking moment just trying to be the best possible employee. Do your work on a high level, but also make sure that you put aside enough time after work to focus on your own dreams. Remember that, by working for someone else, you're only working for salary and your true level of excellence is seldom rewarded the way it should be.

Start separating your own vision from your other professional efforts and make sure that you maintain the kind of excitement about it that will ultimately make it a driving force towards your future. If you're married, you should share your vision with your spouse at the soonest possible opportunity. Even if he or she finds it slightly unusual at first, they will soon realise that you are serious about becoming a FITpreneur and you will find no better support in this world than the assistance of a loving spouse.

Be faithful in your preparation and don't cut any corners. When you start with a certain discipline which is suggested in his book, such as self-hypnosis, make sure that you make it a part of your daily routine. Have you ever seen those people who decide to join the gym because they want to lose weight? Many of them start off at an incredible pace and never miss a day of exercise for the first two weeks. Then, gradually, they go to the gym less often and, eventually, they stopped going altogether. The reason for this is that they never made the mental decision to make daily exercise a part of their permanent routine. They were hoping to see magical results after they joined the gym and, when those results did not materialise, they quickly lost their hope and dedication. It is very important that you do not allow this to happen in your business. Especially during the planning phases, you have to make the mental commitment to creating brand-new thinking patterns in your own mind. You can only do this by dedicating yourself to the mental exercises suggested in this book and by also committing yourself to making them a permanent part of your daily routine. Only then will you ever achieve the kind of restructuring and reprogramming of your mind which will be essential if you hope to ultimately become a FITpreneur.

Rest

Make sure that you get enough rest. It may not be possible for you to get more than four or five hours sleep a night, by reason of your current work commitments, but you should still make sure your body gets the best possible amount of rest during those hours. Don't allow any distractions to steal your rest once you have settled down for a good night's sleep and make sure you obtain the optimum amount of mental and physical rejuvenation possible. You're going to need all of your strength, both mentally and physically, for the journey which lies ahead. It would do you no good to have all of your plans in place, only to fail because you don't have the physical and mental fortitude to make your vision become a reality.

Keep repeating the positive thoughts and reinforcements you have learned about in this book until you truly believe them. Meditate on your vision for the future until you have an absolute certainty that it is going to materialise. Find a way, by using the methods and procedures described in this book, to build a bridge between your mental vision and the concrete reality which you want to experience.

It is time to make your dreams come true and this book has now provided you with all of the practical steps required to facilitate this. Your ultimate success is your own responsibility and the period of time required before you ultimately have your own fitness business will depend entirely on yourself. Now that you have been granted the keys and practical instructions to face you in the right direction, you need to start taking the first steps towards the ultimate attainment of your ideals. Whatever happens, don't ever lose faith in your own abilities and don't allow any setbacks to break your momentum. Everything you need is right there, inside your heart, and as long as you remain faithful and hopeful you will always find a way to keep moving towards your ultimate goal. Believe in yourself and you will find that the universe stands ready to support all of your efforts.

Keep projecting a positive image towards the world and those around you and you will soon discover that the right people will come on board to help make your dreams of becoming a FITpreneur a reality.

Printed in Poland
by Amazon Fulfillment
Poland Sp. z o.o., Wrocław